Under Attack:
The Case Against
Bilingual Education

Also by Stephen Krashen:

Foreign Language Education the Easy Way
Language Education Associates

The Case for Late Intervention: Once a Good Reader, Always a Good Reader
(with Jeff McQuillan)
Language Education Associates

Every Person a Reader:
An Alternative to the California Task Force Report on Reading
Language Education Associates

The Power of Reading
Libraries Unlimited

Fundamentals of Language Education
Laredo Publishing

The Natural Approach
(with Tracy Terrell)
Prentice Hall

Principles and Practice in Second Language Acquisition
Prentice Hall International

On Course: Bilingual Education's Success in California
(with Douglas Biber)
California Association for Bilingual Education

The Input Hypothesis
Laredo Publishing

Writing: Research, Theory and Applications
Laredo Publishing

All of the above titles are available from:

Language Education Associates
P.O. Box 3141
Culver City, CA 90231-3141 U.S.A.

www.LanguageBooks.com
input@LanguageBooks.com

Toll free (US & Canada) 1-800-200-8008
Tel: +1 (310) 568-9338 • Fax: +1 (310) 568-9040

Under Attack:
The Case Against
Bilingual Education

Stephen D. Krashen

1996
Language Education Associates
Culver City, California

Under Attack: The Case Against Bilingual Education

Language Education Associates
Post Office Box 3141
Culver City, CA 90231-3141 U.S.A.

Publisher's Cataloging in Publication
(Prepared by Quality Books Inc.)

Krashen, Stephen D.
   Under attack : the case against bilingual education / Stephen D. Krashen.
   p. cm.
   Includes bibliographical references and index.
   LCCN: 96-77012
   ISBN 0-9652808-2-9

   1. Education, Bilingual.   2. Language acquisition.   3. Language and languages--Study and teaching.   I. Title

LC3731.U5K73 1996   371.97'00973
                                QBI96-20491

Library of Congress Catalog Card Number: 96-77012

Editor: Elan J. Glasser
Typesetting and Printing by Don Bruhnke, Chicago Printing & Embossing Company, Culver City, CA

How to order additional copies of this book:
Copies of this publication are available for $16 each, plus $3 for domestic shipping. (California residents please add 8.25% sales tax.)

Orders may be sent to:
LEA, P.O. Box 3141, Culver City, CA 90231-3141 U.S.A. Fax: (310) 568-9040
Purchase orders are welcome.

Table of Contents

Introduction 1

Chapter 1
The Case for Bilingual Education 3

Chapter 2
A Gradual Exit, Variable Threshold Model
for Limited English Proficient Children 9

Chapter 3
Success Without Bilingual Education? 17

Chapter 4
Does Literacy Transfer? 23

Chapter 5
Socio-Economic Status as
de facto Bilingual Education 33

Chapter 6
Is the Public Against Bilingual Education? 43

Chapter 7
Is English in Trouble? 51

Chapter 8
Inoculating Bilingual Education Against Attack 65

Appendix
Comments on a Recent Critique 73

Index 105

Introduction

Bilingual education is under attack. Letters to the editor, editorials, and talk show hosts repeat the same arguments nearly daily. Bilingual education, they say, doesn't work. Students in bilingual programs do not learn English and those who have never had bilingual education appear to do very well without it. Also, they claim that most parents and teachers don't want it. In addition, there is also the feeling that English is in trouble and that programs such as bilingual education contribute to the erosion of English in the United States.

Even if bilingual education worked, critics argue that it will only work for Spanish, and not for languages that have different writing systems. In addition, they note that there is a severe shortage of qualified bilingual teachers.

In this monograph, I will deal with each of these issues:

- Chapter one is a brief explanation of the principles underlying bilingual education.

- In chapter two I describe one way of applying these principles and also deal with the issue of teacher shortages.

- In chapter three I argue that those who succeeded without bilingual education had, in many cases, "de facto" bilingual education programs, thanks to help from outside of school.

- In chapter four I discuss the issue of whether literacy will transfer to English from languages other than Spanish. My conclusion is that there is strong evidence that it does.

- In chapter five I attempt to explain the success rate of different programs by examining the role of socio-economic status (SES), arguing that high SES provides some of the advantages that a well-organized bilingual education program provides.

- Chapter six examines the issue of attitudes. Are parents and teachers really opposed to bilingual education? It depends on how the question is phrased. In reality, there appears to be surprising support for the principles underlying bilingual education, but there is legitimate concern about application.

• Chapter seven examines the belief that English is in trouble. The evidence is overwhelming that it is not. In fact, primary or "heritage" languages are in trouble, not English.

• In chapter eight I present my own critique of bilingual education. While properly organized bilingual programs are doing well, they could do much better. There is a simple and relatively inexpensive way of improving them: books.

I have also included an appendix, a detailed response to a recent critique of bilingual education that asserts that the research does not support it. I argue that the same studies interpreted as not supporting bilingual education, as well as studies considered methodologically "unacceptable," actually provide support for bilingual education.

Portions of chapter one and all of chapter three were previously published in the *CABE Newsletter*. Chapter two appeared in *NABE News*. A part of chapter four was published in the *CAAPE Newsletter* (California Association of Asian Pacific American Education) and another portion appeared in the *CABE Newsletter*, co-authored with Lorraine Ruiz. The entire chapter was published in *NABE News*. Chapter five was published in *Bilingual Basics*. Chapter six appeared in *NABE News* and portions of the appendix were presented at the Georgetown Round Table for Languages and Linguistics and appeared in *Occasional Papers* of the National Clearinghouse for Bilingual Education. Chapter seven appeared in *Muticultural Education*. I thank Jeff McQuillan and Elan Glasser for their careful reading of the draft of this book and their helpful comments.

Chapter One:
The Case for Bilingual Education

Before presenting the case against bilingual education, it will be helpful to first present the case for bilingual education. Underlying successful bilingual education is the fundamental principle of language acquisition and literacy development: We acquire language by understanding messages, by obtaining comprehensible input (the "input hypothesis"; Krashen, 1994). Similarly, we develop literacy from reading (the reading hypothesis).

When we give children quality education in their primary language, we give them two things:

1. Knowledge, both general knowledge of the world and subject matter knowledge. The knowledge that children get through their first language helps make the English they hear and read more comprehensible. This results in more English language acquisition.

Consider the case of two limited English proficient children. One has had a good education in the primary language, and is well-prepared in math, while the other has not had a good foundation in math. They enter a fourth grade class in which math is taught only in English. Clearly, the child with a good background in math will understand more, and will thus learn more math, and acquire more English, because she is getting more comprehensible input. The child with a poor math background will learn less math and acquire less English.

2. Literacy, which transfers across languages.

Here is a simple, three step argument supporting the transfer of literacy from the first to the second language:

(1) As Frank Smith and Kenneth Goodman have argued, we learn to read by reading, by making sense of what we see on the page (see e.g. Goodman, 1982; Smith, 1994). This hypothesis is very similar to the input hypothesis.

(2) If we learn to read by reading, it will be much easier to learn to read in a language we already understand.

(3) Once you can read, you can read. The ability to read transfers across languages.

Another aspect of literacy transfers as well: The ability to use language to solve problems and thereby grow intellectually. Once, for example, someone can use writing to clarify ideas ("the composing process") in one language, it can be used in any other: Once we are educated, we are educated.

Rossell and Baker (1996) complain that "it is impossible to say why" native language development will help second language development: "there is no underlying psychological mechanism that accounts for the facilitation effect" (p. 31). According to my understanding, knowledge and literacy together make up what Cummins (1981) refers to as "academic language" (formerly CALP). This characterization helps us understand what the advantages are in providing first language support: Knowledge gained through the first language makes English input more comprehensible and literacy gained through the first language transfers to the second.

The Three Components

If the arguments given here are correct, they predict that good bilingual programs will have the following components:

1. Comprehensible input in English, provided directly in the form of ESL and sheltered subject matter classes.[1]

2. Subject matter teaching done in the first language, without translation. This indirect help provides background information that helps makes the English that children read and hear more comprehensible. Methods that use the first language for concurrent translation (the teacher speaking in one language, and then translating what was said into the second language) are not effective in helping children acquire English (Legaretta, 1979, Wong-Fillmore, 1985); when a translation is available, the children do not attend to the input in the second language and teachers do not have to try to make this input comprehensible.

3. Literacy development in the first language, which transfers to the second language.

A fourth very desirable component is the continuation of the development of the primary language. There are good practical reasons (e.g. international business), and cognitive reasons (bilinguals do better on certain linguistic tasks as well as measures of "divergent thinking") to do this. In addition, a high level of competence in the first language contributes to a healthy sense of biculturalism, an avoidance of the state of "bicultural ambivalence," shame of the first culture and rejection of the second culture (Cummins, 1981).

Explaining Bilingual Education: "The Paris Argument"

It is not easy to explain the theory underlying bilingual education to the public. I have had some success, however, with the following analogy. Pretend you have just received, and have accepted, an attractive job offer in Paris. Your French, however, is limited (you had two years of high school French a long time ago). You have also never been to France, and know very little about life in Paris.

Before your departure, the company that is hiring you will send you the following information, in English: What to do when you arrive in Paris, how to get to your hotel, where and how to find a place to live, where to shop, what kinds of schools are available for your children, how French companies function (how people dress in the office, what time work starts and ends, etc.) and specific information about the functioning of the company and your responsibilities.

It would be very useful to get this information right away in English, rather than getting it gradually, as you acquire French. If you get it right away, the world around you will be much more comprehensible, and you will acquire French more quickly.

Anyone who agrees with this, in my opinion, agrees with the philosophy underlying bilingual education.

Russian Language TV and Bilingual Education

A recent article in the Los Angeles Times (June 27, 1995) enthusiastically described a new television station, CRN-TV, which broadcasts, in the Russian language, "a mix of news, political discussion, culture and kids' shows to help acclimatize immigrants to life in the U.S." (p. F-3). CRN-TV has won the support of West Hollywood Mayor John Heilman, who is quoted as saying "CRN has really helped us get the word out to our Russian residents, who make up such a large part of the community. They know about the services we have, and how to report crime, fires, and earthquakes. We're excited to have them in the city." One of the founders of CRN, Michael Kira, states that one of the jobs of CRN is "to bring America into the hearts of everyone who comes here."

It is gratifying that there is such support for an enterprise such as CRN. What is fascinating is that no one seems to object to the fact that the broadcasting is in Russian. Instead, people seem to understand that when immigrants are knowledgeable about the world around them, they adjust more easily, and that providing information in the first language is very efficient.

This is, as noted above, one of the major rationales underlying bilingual education: When we give children subject matter knowledge through the first language, we help them adjust more easily to their new situation, and it makes the instruction they get in English more comprehensible. Because we acquire language by understanding it, this speeds their acquisition of English.

CRN-TV is a very good idea. I am sure that it is a big help in helping Russian immigrants adjust. It can also help their English language development: Someone who is up-to-date on the news, because they have heard it discussed in Russian on CRN, will have an easier time reading English language newspapers and understanding the news on English language television and radio.

(I am not arguing that Russian-language TV is all immigrants need in order to acquire English. They also need comprehensible input in English. But having some background knowledge in Russian will help make this input more comprehensible. Similarly, students in bilingual programs should be, and are, getting comprehensible input in English in addition to subjects taught in the primary language.)

If Russian language television is a good idea, so is bilingual education.

Note

1. In sheltered subject matter classes, intermediate second language acquirers are given comprehensible subject matter instruction in the second language. The focus of the class is on subject matter learning, not language acquisition. Students in these classes typically acquire as much language as students in traditional intermediate classes, and often acquire more, and learn subject matter at the same time (Krashen, 1991).

References

Christon, L. 1995. Educational TV for Russian immigrants. Los Angeles Times, June 27, 1995, p. F-5.

Cummins, J. 1981. The role of primary language development in promoting educational success for language minority students. In Schooling and Language Minority Students. Sacramento, CA: California Department of Education. pp. 3-49.

Goodman, K. 1982. Language and Literacy. London: Routledge and Kegan Paul.

Krashen, S. 1991. Sheltered subject matter teaching. Cross Currents 18: 1 83-1 89.

Krashen, S. and Biber, D. 1988. On Course: Bilingual Education's Success in California. Ontario, CA: California Association for Bilingual Education.

Legarreta, D. 1979. The effects of program models on language acquisition by Spanish-speaking children. TESOL Quarterly 8: 521-576.

Rossell, C. and Baker, K. 1996. The educational effectiveness of bilingual education. Research in the Teaching of English 30: 7-74.

Smith, F. 1994. Understanding Reading. Fifth Edition. Hillsdale, NJ: Erlbaum.

Wong-Fillmore, L. 1985. When does teacher talk work as input? In S. Gass and C. Madden (Eds.) Input in Second Language Acquisition. New York: Newbury House. pp. 17-50.

References

Chapter Two:
A Gradual Exit, Variable Threshold Model for Limited English Proficient Children

Here is one way to set up a program that provides the components for good bilingual programs presented in the previous chapter. Sometimes called the "Eastman plan," it is in wide use in California (table 2.1). We will first deal with an ideal case, where there is a fairly large concentration of children who speak the same first language, and there are faculty trained to work with them.

The plan has three components and four stages. The stages, however, are very flexible. In the beginning stage, all children, limited English proficient and native speakers of English, are mixed for art, music and physical education. This makes sense for two reasons: It avoids segregation and much of the English the minority language children will hear will be comprehensible, thanks to the pictures in art and movement in PE. Also at this stage, children are in high quality comprehensible input-based ESL classes, and are taught all other subjects in the primary language.

The intermediate stage child is defined as the child who understands enough English to begin to learn some content through English. We begin with sheltered subject matter instruction in those subjects that, at this level, do not demand a great deal of abstract use of language, such as math and science. Subjects such as social studies and language arts remain in the first language, as it is more difficult to make these subjects comprehensible to second language acquirers at this level.[1]

At the advanced level, limited English proficient students join the mainstream, but not all at once: They begin with one or two subjects at a time, usually math and science. When this occurs, social studies and language arts can be taught as sheltered subject matter classes.

In the mainstream stage, students do all subjects in the mainstream, and can continue first language development in classes teaching language arts and social studies in the first language. These continuing first language classes are not all-day programs. Rather, they can take the place of (or supplement) foreign language study.

	Table 2.1. **The Gradual Exit Plan**		
	Mainstream	*ESL/Sheltered*	*First Language*
Beginning	Art, Music, PE	ESL	All Core Subjects
Intermediate	Art, Music, PE	ESL, Math, Science	Language Arts, Social Studies
Advanced	Art, Music, PE Math, Science	ESL, Social Studies, Language Arts	Continuing L1 Development
Mainstream	All Subjects		Continuing L1 Development

Examine the possible progress of a limited English proficient student: She does math first in the primary language, then moves to sheltered math, and then finally to the mainstream. At every stage, instruction is comprehensible, and the sheltered class acts as a bridge between the first language class and the mainstream. When she enters the mainstream, this child will know a great deal of math and will be familiar with the special kind of English used in math class.

Gradual Exit

Bilingual educators have been sensitized to the problem of early exit, exiting children from primary language instruction before they are ready (Cummins, 1980). On the other hand, we also have a late exit problem, because we do not always have the resources to provide as much instruction in the first language as we would like to. Our task, therefore, is to make sure we provide primary language instruction where it is most needed.

Of course, some people think there is a different late exit problem: They think that we keep children in primary language instruction too long, after they speak English well enough to be in the mainstream. As Cummins (1980) has pointed out, this is rarely the case. More typically, children have conversational fluency in English but lack academic language ability (literacy and background knowledge), which is efficiently developed in the primary language.

The plan presented here is a gradual exit program: Children are exited into the mainstream gradually, subject by subject, as they are ready to understand the input. The more easily contextualized subjects are the first to be done as sheltered subject matter and are the first to be done in the mainstream.

Note that children never need to exit the bilingual program: They have the option of continuing first language development.

Variable Threshold

Cummins (1981) has suggested that two thresholds exist in first language development. The lower threshold is the minimum amount of first language academic proficiency necessary to make a positive impact on second language academic proficiency. The higher threshold is the amount of first language competence necessary to reap the cognitive benefits of bilingualism.

The task of the bilingual educator is to insure attainment of the lower threshold, and, whenever possible, help students attain the higher threshold. The gradual exit plan accomplishes both of these goals.

The plan employs a "variable threshold" approach for the attainment of the lower threshold: As children reach the threshold for a particular subject matter, they then proceed to follow instruction in English in that subject matter, beginning with sheltered instruction. By providing continuing first language development, the plan also provides for the attainment of the higher threshold and its advantages.

Modifications

As noted earlier, the plan presented above is for the ideal situation. In the less than ideal situation, we attempt to insure that the principles underlying the plan are satisfied, even if the full version cannot be done.

A modified gradual exit plan can be used in situations in which the limited English proficient children speak different first languages and/or primary language instruction is not possible for other reasons (e.g. staffing, materials).

In these cases, two thirds of the plan can be carried out: the "mainstream" and "ESL/sheltered" components. This kind of program has the advantage of being comprehensible all day long, but it lacks the advantages of developing literacy in the first language and using the first language to supply subject matter knowledge. It will be better, however, than ESL "pull-out," which means exposure to incomprehensible input most of the day.

Quite often, however, even the modified plan is not possible. This occurs when there are only a few limited English proficient children in the school, and/or when coordination among teachers is not possible. In cases like this, the classroom teacher can be faced with great diversity within one classroom.

Before discussing some solutions, some ways of reducing the burden, it needs to be pointed out that many teachers today are facing a degree of diversity, of heterogeneity, that has probably never been seen before in the history of education. It is not usual to see a single class with native and fluent English speakers, students who speak no English at all (and who have a poor background in the primary language), and students who speak a wide variety of first languages. Traditional solutions will not work: Even if paraprofessionals are available, teachers must supervise them, and wind up making two, three or even four lesson plans every period. Bilingual teachers sometimes must translate simply to get through the period, an exhausting procedure that does not result in second language acquisition. And we wonder why teachers burn out so quickly! The real solution is to set up a plan similar to the gradual exit plan, with team-teaching. But let us consider the situation in which this is not possible. We will return to the principles underlying successful programs and see to what extent we can work toward them in this situation.

Submersion and Pull-out ESL

Even in submersion situations, we can mimic the gradual exit plan to some extent. Of course, the art, music and PE parts of the day will be the same regardless of whether the full plan can be used or not: the children will be together for this part of the day. Comprehensible-input based ESL can be of great help, even if it is done on a pull-out basis. The time to pull out the limited English speakers is the time of day when more proficient English speakers are doing the subject matter that requires the most abstract use of language and that will be the least comprehensible for the new second language acquirer: language arts and social studies.

When beginners in English are submersed in classes with more proficient English speakers, we can make life easier on them and us, and help their language acquisition by being consistent with the concept of comprehensible input, e.g. by allowing a silent period, gently encouraging but not forcing production in early stages of second language acquisition, and when the children do begin to speak, by not insisting on complete sentences and not correcting errors (Krashen and Terrell, 1983). If the teacher understands some of the child's first language, there is no reason not to utilize the natural approach procedure of allowing the child to respond in the first language. This will greatly facilitate communication.

Primary Language Development without Bilingual Education

Home use of the first language

When primary language instruction is not possible, there is still a great deal that can be done to get some of the positive effects of bilingual education. First, we can encourage the use of the first language at home. Parents often ask if they should use more English at home, thinking that this will speed up English language development in their children. Unless the parent speaks English extremely well, switching to English has the danger of disturbing parent-child communication, which cripples both cognitive and emotional development (Wong-Fillmore, 1991). This view is confirmed by the research. Several studies show that when parents switch to exclusive use of the language of the country, school performance suffers (Cummins, 1981; Dolson, 1985). This practice also seems not to benefit English language development (Ramirez and Politzer, 1975). We would much rather teach a child in kindergarten who does not speak English but who is well-adjusted and ready for school than a child who has picked up some English (from an imperfect model) but who has not been communicating very well with his parents.

Helpers

Another way we can make use of the first language without a full bilingual program is the judicious use of paraprofessionals and other helpers. All too often, these helpers are used to drill English spelling and vocabulary. If we have a helper who speaks the child's first language, we should use that helper to provide background knowledge and literacy in the child's first language. This help will usually be most effective in those subjects requiring the most use of abstract language: social studies and language arts.

Even when only a little help is available, it can be very valuable. Consider the case of a class with three Korean speaking children, who know little English. They are progressing fairly well in mathematics, because of their good background in their first language, and because math does not require a high level of language ability in early grades. Social studies, however, is more difficult for them. Assume that a paraprofessional who speaks Korean is available only one morning per week for one hour. My suggestion is that we inform the helper what will take place the following week in social studies. If it is the civil war, the helper uses the one hour on Monday to provide the children with background information, in Korean, about the civil war: Who the combattants were, what the issues were, etc.. This will make the history lessons that follow during the week much more comprehensible.

Classmates who speak the limited English proficient child's first language can help and sometimes do spontaneously. We should allow this to occur: It is not a good policy to forbid the use of the first language in school: "English only" rules are not good for English. Peer help should be done the same way we do it in bilingual education programs: As a source of background information and academic knowledge in the first language, not as on-line translation.

First language use in class

There is also nothing wrong with an occasional translation in class. Teachers need not waste time in frustrating pantomine and paraphrase when a concept is important, explanation of its meaning resists normal efforts and the teacher or another student can explain the concept quickly in the child's first language. The problem occurs when input is so hard to understand that translation is no longer occasional but becomes concurrent translation.

Books in the primary language

When some books are provided in the primary language, in the classroom and school libraries, they help validate the primary language and culture, can contribute to continued first language development, and can help literate students get subject matter knowledge. Feuerverger (1994) noted that children who made greater use of books in the first language provided by the school had "a greater feeling of security in their cultural background" (p. 143).

Staffing

There are short-term and long term solutions to the bilingual teacher shortage, and the gradual exit plan can help with both.

First, the plan provides some immediate relief. Because it is gradual exit and does not require full development of all aspects of academic language in the primary language before transition begins, it requires fewer teachers who can teach in the primary language. Second, the gradual exit plan is well-suited to team-teaching, with those who speak the child's first language teaching in the primary language, and with those who do not teaching in the mainstream and sheltered/ESL sections. I have occasionally witnessed a bilingual teacher teaching a class in English, and, at the same time, down the hall, noticed that there was a non-bilingual who has had a year of Spanish class and a few months in Mexico struggling through a lesson in Spanish. Clearly, there is an easier way. In my view, if a teacher speaks the child's first language well, he or she needs to teach in that language as much as possible, even if that teacher speaks English perfectly. Many bilingual teachers have told me that they are willing to do this; in fact, it makes their day easier.

This kind of team-teaching will make life easier for English-language teachers as well. Their limited English proficient students, thanks to their good background knowledge and literacy competence, developed in the first language, will be much easier to teach.

A long-term strategy for reducing the teacher shortage is to encourage the continuing development of the primary language, as is done in the gradual exit plan. As noted earlier, there are very good reasons for doing this, including practical and cognitive reasons. An additional reason is that at least some of the students currently enrolled in bilingual programs will be interested in becoming bilingual teachers. This plan can help them develop the linguistic competence to do so. We can, in other words, grow our own.

Notes

1. When the limited English proficient children reach the intermediate stage, we might consider additional mixing of children: English speakers could make occasional visits to ESL classes to join in selected activities. In addition, if a school offers Spanish as a second language, Spanish speakers could visit the SSL classes to provide some peer input.

Here is an example. Assume that the ESL class is doing an activity such as "The Desert Island" (Christison and Bassano, 1981), in which students, in small groups, discuss what supplies they would take with them if they were stranded on a desert island. Native speakers of English make their strongest contribution in such an activity simply by participating in the groups with the ESL students. The activity constrains the discourse, which helps makes input more comprehensible.

Such careful mixing has several advantages. First, it helps the children get to know each other. Second, it is very likely that the Spanish speakers will make faster progress in English than the English speakers will make in Spanish. This will certainly have a positive effect on the self-esteem of the Spanish speakers and inspire some respect for them in the eyes of the English speaking children.

References

Christison, M. and Bassano, S. 1981. Look Who's Talking. San Francisco: Alta.

Cummins, J. 1980. The exit and entry fallacy in bilingual education. NABE Journal 4: 25-60.

Cummins, J. 1981. The role of primary language development in promoting educational success for language minority students. In Schooling and Language Minority Students. Sacramento, CA: California Department of Education. pp. 3-49.

Dolson, D. 1985. The effects of Spanish home language use on the scholastic performance of Hispanic pupils. Joumal of Multilingual and Multicultural Development 6: 135-155.

Feuerverger, G. 1994. A multicultural literacy intervention for minority language students. Language and Education 8:123-146.

Krashen, S. 1991. Sheltered subject matter teaching. Cross Currents 18: 183-189.

Krashen, S. and Terrell, T. 1983. The Natural Approach: Language Acquisition in the Classroom. New York: Prentice Hall.

Ramirez, A. and Politzer, R. 1975. The acquisition of English and the maintenance of Spanish in a bilingual education program. TESOL Quarterly 9:113-124.

Wong Fillmore, L. 1991. When learning a second language means losing the first. Early Childhood Research Quarterly 6: 323-346.

Chapter Three:
Success Without Bilingual Education?

A popular argument against bilingual education is the claim that success is possible without it. There is no doubt that this is true - some people have done well without bilingual education. In cases in which this has occured, however, the conditions underlying successful bilingual education programs have been met, either outside of school or in school, and in many cases a de facto bilingual education program was provided.

In this chapter, I examine cases of "success without bilingual education," individuals who succeeded in acquiring the second language and succeeded in school. While some of them have been presented as counterevidence to bilingual education, my interpretation is that they count as evidence for bilingual education.

Case Histories: Late-Comers

Grace Cho: Born in Korea, Grace Cho's family moved to Argentina when she was school age. In school, she was faced with a total submersion situation; schools in Argentina make no provision for limited Spanish-speaking students – there were no Spanish as a second language classes, no sheltered classes, and there was no bilingual education. Nevertheless, she succeeded; she acquired Spanish very well, did well in school, and today, in Los Angeles, works as a bilingual (Spanish-English) teacher.

The conditions underlying successful bilingual education were satisfied outside of school in this case. The first factor is her previous schooling. Unlike so many limited English proficient children who arrive in the US, when Cho arrived in Argentina, she was at or above "grade level," and was a success in school in Korea. Thus, she already had considerable subject matter knowledge and literacy development.

Second, her parents hired tutors for her immediately, tutors who worked with her in Korean, primarily helping her with subject matter, and helping her Korean language competence to continue to develop. In other words, her parents made sure that the second and third characteristics of good bilingual education, subject matter instruction in the primary language and development of literacy in the primary language, were present. Cho reports that because of this help, her school work was much more comprehensible, and this helped her acquire Spanish more easily.

Fernando de la Pena: de la Pena (1991) presents several cases of immigrants who, he claims, "made it" without bilingual education. One is his own case: Although he was born in El Paso, he spent his first eight years in Mexico, and came to the US at age nine with no English competence. He reports that he acquired English rapidly, and "by the end of my first school year, I was among the top students" (p. 19). A closer look at his case shows that de la Pena had the advantages of bilingual education: In Mexico, he was in the fifth grade, and was thus literate in Spanish and knew subject matter. In addition, when he started school in the US he was put back two grades and placed in grade three (no wonder he was at the top of his class!). His superior knowledge of subject matter helped make the English input he heard more comprehensible.

Mai: A second case described by de la Pena is Mai, a Vietnamese immigrant who came to the United States as an adult. "When Mai first arrived in the U.S., she found a job within two weeks with the American Red Cross" (p. 68). Mai had studied English in Vietnam, had used it in her work there, and had earned a degree in social work. Mai had had all three components of a successful bilingual education program when she arrived in the United States: Knowledge, gained through her first language, literacy in her first language, and competence in English.

Cynthia: Now a successful investment analyst, Cynthia, also described in de la Pena (1991), came to the US at age 12 from Hong Kong at grade level, and with six years of English study in a British school behind her in Hong Kong. Even so, "it took her a good nine months to pick up enough English in class before she could attempt to answer the teacher's questions" (p. 76), two years until she was "comfortable" with English and ten years until she was "confident" (p. 77)! Even after graduating high school, on her first job, "she was baited and insulted by one of her superiors, who told her that her English was hard to understand. 'Where the heck did you learn how to speak and write so strangely?' he asked her mockingly" (p. 77). Cynthia's case shows that even with all the advantages she had, second language acquisition does not happen overnight.

These four cases are very different from many of the children we see in school today, children of poverty who do not have a good education in the primary language, who were not at grade level in their own country, and who did not have high levels of first language literacy.

Starting in Kindergarten

What about children who either grow up in the United States or arrive at kindergarten, and who do not speak English at the time they enter school? The best known of these cases is Richard Rodriguez, who tells his own story in his book *Hunger of Memory*. We know that Rodriguez did, in fact, develop a very high level of English literacy, and that he did not participate in any special programs. He did, however, grow up in an English-speaking neighborhood in Sacramento, and was the only Spanish-speaker in his class. Although he gives us little detail about his social life, it is likely that he received a considerable amount of comprehensible input from his classmates and friends.

While he developed conversational language from interaction, Rodriguez developed academic language by becoming a voracious reader, ("I entered high school having read hundreds of books. My habit of reading made me a confident speaker and writer of English." (p. 63), a route not available to many limited English proficient children because of lack of access to books (Krashen, 1993, Pucci, 1994).

An Empirical Study

Turner, Laria, Shapiro and Perez (1993) also present evidence that strongly suggests that those who do well without bilingual education or special programs have often had a good foundation in the first language. They contrasted 19 Latino college students with 16 Latino high school dropouts of the same age. The found no significant differences between the groups in socio-economic status (both groups were of low SES), and no difference in level of stress reported in their lives. There was also no difference in general intelligence, as measured by the Wechsler Adult Intelligence Scale block design subtest, but the college group was significantly better in the digit symbol test, which reflects academic experiences. Surprisingly, the amount of family transiency and the frequency of working outside of school were higher in the college group.

Of great interest to us is the finding that the college students came to the US at a later age (mean 7.16 years, compared to 2.81) and significantly more of them reported schooling outside the United States, 52.6%, compared to 18.8% of the drop-outs. Although there was no difference reported between in the groups in participation in bilingual or special programs, my view is that 52.6% of the college students had two out of three of the components of bilingual education outside the United States, developing literacy and subject matter knowledge in their first language, and this contributed to their school success. (See Ferris and Politzer, 1981, for similar conclusions.)

Asians and Hispanics

It is frequently claimed that Asian students tend to be very successful while Hispanic students are less successful. Many Asian students, it is pointed out, arrive in the fourth grade with no English, and by the time they are in the sixth grade they are at the top of the class.

Similar observations are presented in the Little Hoover Commission's report:

"A woman with 15 years experience as an Hispanic aide in an English-as-a-Second Language Program ... told the Commission of the disparity she had seen between Hispanic children who were taught in their native language and Asian refugees ("boat people") who were taught in English. 'The children from the Orient were learning how to speak English, without being taught in their own language ... The (Hispanic) children were not progressing. They instead were confused by being taught in their native Spanish language and being forced to try to learn English after the fact. I was truly amazed when I encountered the Oriental children learning their reading, writing and arithmetic in English without so much as a hint there was a language barrier. I asked myself, 'Why can't my kids do that?'" (p. 25).

Not all Asian students do this well, however. Many of our students from Cambodia and Laos, for example, come without a great deal of schooling in the first language, and do not excel in our schools. It is quite true that many Spanish speaking students have problems in school; typically, they do not have a good foundation in the first language. We also, however, have Spanish-speaking children in our schools who are well-educated in the first language. They come in the fourth grade with no English and by the time they are in the sixth grade, they are at the top of the class.

The crucial variable is not Asian-Hispanic. The crucial variable here is the quality of the child's education in the primary language. Children who come with a good education in the first language have two of the three characteristics of a good program already: They have subject matter knowledge in the first language and literacy development in the first language. The curriculum, even when it is in English, is far more comprehensible for them than for children without a good education in the primary language. In fact, these well-educated children are excellent advertisements for bilingual education.

Conclusion

Success without bilingual education is possible, of course. Success without comprehensible input is not possible, however, and apparent cases of success without bilingual education all received comprehensible input. They also, in many cases, had a de facto bilingual education program which helped make the English input they heard and read more comprehensible.

A problem with the argument presented here is that one cannot possibly discuss every case. In addition, potential counterexamples are often presented with very little detail. People often claim that someone they knew succeeded without special programs, but we rarely know what really went on, nor do we always know to what level the person acquired English literacy. Nevertheless, we can conclude that for the cases for which some description is available, comprehensible input was provided, and the first language was often used in a way that made input more comprehensible.

References

de la Pena, F. 1991. Democracy or Babel? The Case for Official English. Washington, DC: US English .

Ferris, M. and Politzer, R. 1981. Effects of early and delayed second language acquisition: English composition skills of Spanish-speaking junior high school students. TESOL Quarterly 15: 263-274.

Krashen, S. 1993. The Power of Reading. Englewood, CO: Libraries Unlimited.

Little Hoover Commission 1993. A Chance to Succeed: Providing English Learners with Supportive Education. Sacramento, CA: Commission on California State Government Organization and Economy.

Pucci, S. 1994. Supporting Spanish language literacy: Latino children and free reading resources in schools. Bilingual Research Journal 18: 67-82.

Rodriguez, R. 1983. Hunger of Memory. New York: Bantam.

Turner, C., Laria, A., Shapiro, E. and Perez, M. 1993. Poverty, resilience, and academic achievement among Latino college students and high school dropouts. In R. Rivera and S. Nieto (Eds.) The Education of Latino Students in Massachusetts: Issues, Research, and Policy Implications. Boston: University of Massachusetts Press. pp. 191-216.

Chapter Four: Does Literacy Transfer?

A major principle of bilingual education is that literacy transfers across languages: If a child learns how to read in one language, that child knows how to read, and that general ability will facilitate learning to read in another language.

The existence of transfer has been questioned. Porter (1990) claims that there is a lack of evidence supporting transfer. In addition, she states that "even if there were a demonstrable advantage for Spanish-speakers learning to read first in their home language, it does not follow that the same holds true for speakers of languages that do not use the Roman alphabet" (p. 65).

In this chapter, I argue that there is a reasonable amount of evidence, direct and indirect, supporting the transfer hypothesis. Specifically, studies show that:

1. the underlying process of reading in different languages is similar, even when the languages and writing systems appear to be very different;

2. the process of the development of literacy is similar in different languages.

Points (1) and (2) allow the possibility of transfer. If the process of reading and the development of literacy were completely different in different languages, it would be unlikely that transfer was possible. If transfer did exist, we would expect points (3) and (4) to be true:

3. when confounding factors are controlled, there are positive correlations between literacy development in first and second languages;

4. bilingual programs in which children develop literacy in the primary language are successful in helping children develop literacy in English.

In this chapter, I briefly summarize the evidence for points 1,2 and 3 (point 4 has been discussed extensively in the professional literature; see e.g. Willig, 1985; Krashen and Biber, 1988; see also the appendix to this volume).

1. The underlying process of reading in different languages is similar.

Evidence for this conclusion comes from studies of miscue analysis, predictors of reading scores, eye-fixation research, and reading strategies.

Miscue analysis: The major result of miscue analysis (Goodman, 1979) is that readers use semantic and syntactic cues to construct meaning, in addition to graphomorphemic (print) cues. In other words, readers do not simply "recode" letters into sounds and then interpret the resultant oral language. Their errors, or "miscues," show that they make predictions about the text they are reading based on previous knowledge, their knowledge of language, and the graphemic system, and use minimum visual information to confirm these guesses.

When a reader, for example, reads "there was a glaring spotlight." instead of the text "There were glaring spotlights." (example from Goodman, 1979), it is evidence that "the reader is processing language, he is not just saying the names of words" (p. 6): This reader has made a prediction about the sentence, has used his knowledge of language to predict its form, and has confirmed its form using only some of the visual information available. His miscue is evidence of an efficient reading process.

Goodman (1973) has proposed that the process of reading is fundamentally the same is all languages except for "minor degrees" of difference (p. 26). So far, research has confirmed that Goodman is correct. Barrera (1981) and Hudelson (1981) have shown that Spanish readers make similar miscues, while Romatowki (1981) and Hodes (1981) reported similar data for readers of Polish and Yiddish, respectively. The latter finding is especially interesting because Yiddish does not use the Roman alphabet; Yiddish uses the Hebrew alphabet even though it is a Germanic language.

In addition, readers of Chinese as a first language show evidence of using the same reading process. Chang, Hung and Tzeng (1982) performed a miscue analysis of the oral reading of third and fourth grade "normal" and "disabled" readers in Taiwan and reported that their subjects produced the same kinds of miscues as readers in other languages. In addition, in agreement with research using other languages, better readers made fewer miscues, showed evidence of processing larger units, and tended to make more semantically and syntactically acceptable miscues (see e.g. Devine, 1981).

Predictors of reading scores: Stevenson, Stigler, Lucker and Lee (1982) reported that similar factors predicted good reading in very different languages. For fifth graders in Japan, Taiwan, and the United States, the amount of general information the children knew was a significant factor in predicting reading scores. Contrary to what one might expect, ability to do spatial relations and perceptual speed did not play a special role in predicting reading scores for Chinese and Japanese children; rather, verbal abilities were more important. Stevenson et. al. concluded that their results suggest that " ... the dominant problem (in learning to read) is that of abstracting meaning from an abstract set of symbols, and the characteristics of the orthography play a less critical role than has sometimes been proposed" (p. 1179). This conclusion is consistent with the hypothesis that the process of learning to read is universal.

Eye-fixation: Gray (1956, cited in Just and Carpenter, 1987) examined eye fixation and reading speed among native speakers of 14 different languages, including Arabic, English, Hebrew, Burmese, Chinese, Urdu, Navaho, and Yoruba. He found that despite the differences in orthographies, the average number of fixations per word was very similar, and concluded that "fluent reading is roughly similar across languages and orthographies" (Just and Carpenter, p. 306).

In a more detailed study, Just, Carpenter, and Wu (1983; cited in Just and Carpenter, 1987), compared eye-fixations of Chinese speakers reading scientific texts in Chinese with data from native speakers of English. They also concluded that despite the differences in orthographies, the two languages "are processed by similar types of mechanisms and they ultimately result in similar representations of the text content" (Just and Carpenter, p. 314).

Just et. al. found that as in English, there was a clear relationship between Chinese word frequency and how long the Chinese readers looked at the word, suggesting similar mechanisms for lexical access. In addition, gaze duration was longer when a Chinese word contained more characters, and gaze duration for individual characters was longer for characters that contained more individual componenets (strokes). This is similar to findings in English showing longer fixations for longer words.

Development of writing: A number of studies in English support the hypothesis that writing style is a result of reading (Krashen, 1993). Lee (1995) found evidence that this is also the case in Chinese, reporting a clear relationship between the amount of pleasure reading done and scores of the essay portion of a national examination taken by high school students in Taiwan.

Reading strategies: There is good evidence that readers use similar strategies in learning to read different languages. Consistent with children learning to read in English, children learning to read in Dutch, whether as a first or second language, have less difficulty with words with CVC (consonant-vowel-consonant) patterns than words with CC clusters, had less trouble with monosyllabic words than bisyllabic words, and were better at reading familiar than unfamiliar words (Verhoeven, 1990).

Similar strategies for deriving meaning from text are used in different languages. Carpenter and Just (1975) asked English and Chinese speakers to read sentences such as:

(1) It's true that the dots are red.
(2) It's true that the dots are not red.

in their own language, while showing them pictures of red and black dots. Subjects were asked if the sentences they read were true or false. There were four possible combinations:

(a) The subject sees red dots, reads sentence (1).
(b) The subject sees black dots, reads sentence (1).
(c) The subject sees red dots, reads sentence (2).
(d) The subject sees black dots, reads sentence (2).

For both languages, reaction times were the same: Subjects responded to sentences similar to (a) the fastest, and then types (b), (c), and (d) in order. Reaction times in English and Chinese, moreover, were nearly identical. Carpenter and Just reported similar results with Norwegian speaking subjects reading in Norwegian, using slightly different stimuli.[1]

Finally, Just et. al. reported that summaries of texts that Chineses and English readers produced are similar: "both groups recalled more of the high-level important information and fewer of the details and elaborations" (Just and Carpenter, p. 313).

2. The process of the development of literacy is similar in different languages.

Studies supporting the generalization that learning to read is similar in different languages include studies of vocabulary acquisition, the print environments of good and poor readers, and cases of literacy development without instruction.

Vocabulary acquisition: Research in vocabulary development reveals clear similarities between English and other languages. Studies with English readers have shown that readers show small, but significant gains in word knowledge even after a single exposure to an unfamiliar word in context (Nagy, Herman and Anderson, 1985). Similar findings have been reported for reading Chinese as a first language (Shu, Anderson and Zhang, 1994) and French as a second language (Dupuy and Krashen, 1993).

Good versus poor readers: Better English readers tend to live in more print-rich environments (research reviewed in Krashen, 1993). The same appears to be true with other languages: Chang and Tzeng (1992) reported that "disabled" or nonproficient beginning readers in Chinese "had their very first and only experience with Chinese print through school textbooks" (p. 28).

Literacy development without instruction: There are also anecdotal reports of readers who have succeeded in improving their level of Chinese literacy by reading, without instruction, paralleling similar cases in English (Krashen, 1993). J.L. immigrated to the United States at age 11 and J.W. came at age 12. Both continued their habit of pleasure reading in Chinese, their first language. Now university students, they both report that their Chinese literacy level has grown. J.L. reports that she used the dictionary at first in reading Chinese, but no longer needs it, while J.W. reports that " ... due to my habit of reading Chinese comic books, I can now recognize many Chinese characters ... that I did not learn in elementary school when I was in Taiwan."

3. When confounding factors are controlled, there are positive correlations between literacy development in first and second languages.

Studies attempting to simply show correlations between first language reading ability and second language reading ability have not shown consistent results (e.g. Trager and Wong, 1984). This is because the relationship between the first and the second language can be influenced by length of exposure to the second language; as children stay in a country longer, their second language proficiency will increase, while their first language reading proficiency may decrease, due to lack of first language printed input (Cummins, Swain, Nakajima, Handscombe, Green and Tran, 1984). In studies in which both languages are allowed to develop, or there is control for length of residence and/or age, relationships between first and second language literacy are typically positive.

First language reading has been shown to be a good predictor of second language reading ability for a wide variety of languages, including:

1) Chinese as a first language, English as a second language (Hoover, 1983);

2) Japanese as a first language, English as a second language (Cummins et. al., 1984);

3) Vietnamese as a first language, English as a second language (Cummins et. al., 1984);

4) Turkish as a first language, Dutch as a second language (Bossers, 1991; Verhoeven, 1991a, 1991 b);

5) Spanish as a first language, English as a second language (Carroll, 1991);

6) English as a first language, Spanish as a second language (Carroll, 1991);

7) English as a first language, French as a second language (Swain, Lapkin and Barik, 1976).

In summary, there is very good evidence that reading in all languages is done in a similar way and acquired in a similar way. Moreover, those who read well in the first language tend to read well in their second language. This data provides very strong support for Cummins' contention that a "common underlying proficiency" exists, that literacy development in one language provides a clear advantage in developing literacy in any other language (e.g. Cummins, 1981).

Seeing Transfer Happen

I have presented a theoretical argument for the transfer of literacy. Such abstract evidence, however, is not as powerful as actually seeing it happen. In Lorraine Ruiz's second grade class, transfer clearly took place.

Ms. Ruiz' class consisted of 33 students: All were Spanish speakers and only three of their parents spoke English. All but one of the students were classified as limited or non-English speaking. Nearly the entire curriculum was taught in Spanish, including reading, which was done with a "whole language thematic approach" with "a little dab of phonics." Ms. Ruiz read to the class frequently, both in Spanish and English, but the only English input the children had in class was aural.

Ms. Ruiz included 20 minutes per day of a free choice activity; one of the options was to spend time in the classroom library, which included books in both Spanish and English. From the beginning, Ms. Ruiz noticed that the English books were more popular with the children. This was because there were more of them, and because the English books were of higher quality than the Spanish books.

At the beginning of the school year, the reading of the English books was completely "pretend" reading, with the child looking at the pictures and "reading" the story outloud in Spanish. But by the end of the year, the children were clearly reading the English books with good comprehension, and nearly all reading was real reading. The children were quite amazed at their ability to read in English. One child asked Ms. Ruiz, "When did you teach us to read in

English?" The answer, of course, is that Ms. Ruiz helped them learn to read in Spanish, and once you can read, you can read.

Of course, a more rigorous study could be done to tally the actual amount of English reading done and the actual degree of comprehension could be probed. But Ms. Ruiz' experience is not an isolated one. In fact, this kind of transfer is reported very frequently. Literacy really does transfer across languages.

Note

1. While some processing operations appear to be universal, others may be language-specific. In English, for example, the subject is typically the first noun in the sentence, that is, English uses a word order strategy. In other languages, other strategies are more important. In Dutch morphological cues take precedence over word order (McDonald, 1987). In a sentence such as "Him saw I," English speakers tend to consider "him" as the subject, while Dutch speakers would consider "I" as the subject. There is good evidence, however, that while second language acquirers may initially use their first language preferences when interpreting sentences in the second language, over time they acquire the second language strategies (McDonald, 1987; Gass, 1987; Harrington, 1987).

References

Barrera, R. 1981. Reading in Spanish: Insights from children's miscues. In: S. Hudelson (Ed.) Learning to Read in Different Languages. Washington: Center for Applied Linguistics. pp 1-9.

Bossers, B. 1991. On thresholds, ceilings and short-circuits: The relation between L1 reading, L2 reading and L2 knowledge. AILA Review 8: 45-60.

Carpenter, M. and Just, P. 1975. Sentence comprehension: A psycholinguistic processing model of verification. Psychological Review 82: 45-73.

Carrell, P. 1991. Second language reading: Reading ability or language proficiency? Applied Linguistics 12: 159-179.

Chang, J-M.and Tzeng, O. 1992. Reading ability and disability among Chinese beginning readers: Implications for educators. In P. Hackett, X. Yu and L. Zhang (Eds.), Proceedings of Chinese Education for the 21st Century Conference. Charlottesville: University of Virginia, Curry School of Education. pp. 23-31.

Chang, J-M, Hung, D., and Tzeng, O. 1992. Miscue analysis of Chinese children's reading behavior at the entry level. Journal of Chinese Linguistics 20: 119-158.

Cummins, J. 1981.The role of primary language development in promoting success for language minority students. In Schooling and Language Minority Students: A Theoretical Framework. Edited by Office of Bilingual Bicultural Education, State of California. Los Angeles: Evaluation, Dissemination and Assessment Center, California State University. pp. 3-49.

Cummins, J., Swain, M., Nakajima, K., Handscombe, J., Geen, D. and Tran, C. 1984. Linguistic interdependence among Japanese and Vietnamese immigrant students. In C. Rivera (Ed.) Communicative Competence Approaches to Language Proficiency Assessment: Research and Application. Clevedon, Avon: Multilingual Matters. pp. 60-81.

Devine, J. 1981. Developmental patterns in native and non-native reading acquisition. In S. Hudelson (Ed.) Learning to Read in Different Languages. Washington: Center for Applied Linguistics. pp.103-114.

Dupuy, B. and Krashen, S. 1993. Incidental vocabulary acquisition in French as a foreign language. Applied Language Learning 4: 55-63.

Gass, S. 1987. The resolution of conflicts among competing systems: A bidirectional approach. Applied Psycholinguistics 8: 329-350.

Goodman, K. 1973. Psycholinguistic universals in the reading process. In F. Smith (Ed.) Psycholinguistics and Reading. New York: Holt Rinehart and Winston. pp. 21-27.

Goodman, K. 1979. Miscues: Windows on the reading process. In K. Goodman (Ed.) Miscue Analysis: Applications to Reading Instruction. Urbana, Illinois: ERIC. pp. 3-14.

Harrington, M. 1987. Processing transfer: Language-specific processing strategies as a source of interlanguage variation. Applied Psycholinguistics 8: 351-377.

Hodes, P. 1981. Reading: A universal process. In S. Hudelson (Ed.) Learning to Read in Different Languages. Washington, DC: Center for Applied Linguistics. pp. 27-31.

Hoover, W..1983. Language and Literacy Learning in Bilingual Education. Austin, Texas: Southwest Educational Development Laboratory.

Hudelson, S. 1981. An investigation of the oral reading behaviors of native Spanish speakers. In S. Hudelson (Ed.) Learning to Read in Different Languages. Washington, DC: Center for Applied Linguistics. pp. 10-20.

Just, M. and Carpenter, M. 1987. The Psychology of Reading and Language Comprehension. Boston: Allyn and Bacon.

Krashen, S. 1993. The Power of Reading. Englewood, Colorado: Libraries Unlimited.

Krashen, S. and Biber, D. 1988. On Course: Bilingual Education's Success in Califomia. Ontario, CA: California Association for Bilingual Education.

Lee, S-Y. 1995. A cross-cultural validation of the reading hyothesis: The relationship of pleasure reading to writing proficiency and academic achievement among Taiwanese senior high school students. PhD dissertation, School of Education, University of Southern California.

McDonald, J. 1987. Sentence interpretation in bilingual speakers of English and Dutch. Applied Psycholinguistics 8: 379-413.

Nagy, W., Herman, P., and Anderson, R. 1985. Learning words from context. Reading Research Quarterly 20: 233-253.

Nagy, W. and Herman, P. 1987. Breadth and depth of vocabulary knowledge: Implications for acquisition and instruction. In M. McKeown and M. Curtis (Eds.) The Nature of Vocabulary Acquisition. Hillsdale, NJ: Erlbaum. pp. 19-35.

Porter, R. 1990. Forked Tongue. New York: Basic Books.

Romatowski, J. 1981. A study of oral reading in Polish and English. In S. Hudelson (Ed.) Learning to Read in Different Languages. Washington: Center for Applied Linguistics. pp. 21-26.

Shu, H., Anderson, R. and Zhang, H. 1995. Incidental learning of word meanings while reading: A Chinese and American cross-cultural study. Reading Research Quarterly 30: 76-95.

Smith, F. 1994 Understanding Reading. Hillsdale, NJ: Erlbaum.

Stevenson, H., Stigler, J., Lucker, G., Lee, S., Hsu, C. and Kitamura, S. 1982. Reading disabilities: The case of Chinese, Japanese, and English. Child Development 53:1164-1181.

Swain, M., Lapkin, S., and Barik, H. 1976. The cloze test as a measure of second language proficiency for young children. Working Papers on Bilingualism 11: 32-42.

Trager, B. and Wong, B.K. 1984. The relationship between native and second language reading comprehension and second language oral ability. In C. Rivera (Ed.) Placement Procedures in Bilingual Education: Education and Policy Issues. Clevedon, England: Multilingual Matters.

Verhoeven, L. 1990. Acquisition of reading in a second language. Reading Research Quarterly 25: 90-114.

Verhoeven, L. 1991a. Predicting minority children's bilingual proficiency: Child, family, and institutional factors. Language Learning 41: 205-233.

Verhoeven, L. 1991b. Acquisition of literacy. AILA Review 8: 61-74.

Willig, A. 1985. A meta-analysis of selected studies on the effectiveness of bilingual education. Review of Educational Research 55: 269-317.

Chapter Five: Socio-Economic Status as de facto Bilingual Education

Socio-economic status has been shown to be a consistent predictor of student success. Of special interest here is that studies of language minority students have found SES to be a strong predictor of school success, independent of the effects of first language (Rosenthal, Milne, Ellman, Ginsburg, and Baker, 1983; McArthur, 1993).

In this chapter, I discuss, and to some extent re-analyze, data from three reports on the success of language minority students, and argue that in each case socio-economic status plays a clear role. At no time do I argue that SES is the only determinant of academic success. I will argue that socio-economic factors should not be ignored, and that examining why high SES is correlated with success in school may help us design better programs.

Study 1: Toronto

Cummins (1984) presents data from surveys conducted in 1969 and 1975 by the Toronto Board of Education on placement of students in "High Academic" programs (college preparatory). SES classification was based on parents' occupation and all children were in English-only programs. As Cummins points out, there were large differences among language minority groups: A much larger percentage of students who spoke Chinese as a first language was included in the high academic program, even compared to native speakers of English, regardless of SES. Nevertheless, SES played a clear role.

Table 5.1, from Cummins' table 4, confirms that there is little difference between native and non-native speakers of English in academic success when SES is controlled. Among low SES immigrant language minority children, nearly half were in the college preparatory stream, a higher percentage than Canadian-born native speakers of English, while for language minority students born in Canada, an even higher percentage of low SES children were in the high academic program. Figures for higher SES students are similar.

Table 5.1.
**Percent of Students in High Academic (College Preparatory)
Program (1979 data)**

First Language	Low SES	High SES	d	r
Not English: Born in Canada	62% (2163/3489)	75% (2357/3158)	.28	.14
Not English: Born outside Canada	48% (2170/4521)	67% (1995/2971)	.11	.06
English: Born in Canada	40% (1182/4270)	67% (6276/9270)	.87	.40

from: Cummins, 1984

But SES had an effect. According to my calculations, the difference between the percentage of low SES and high SES students in the high academic program was significant (for first language not English, born in Canada, chi square = 121.73; for first language not English, born outside Canada, chi square = 21.34; for native speakers of English, chi square = 1892.47; in all cases df = 1). All these differences were easily statistically significant, because of the large sample size. Effect sizes, however, were small (computed from chi squares; see table 5.1, using Johnson, 1989), except for the native speakers of English (r = .40).

My presentation differs from Cummins' table 4; in that table, low SES students are compared with all students, which includes the low SES group. In table 5.1, I compare low SES to the other students, not including the low SES group, which highlights the effect of SES.

As Cummins notes, SES is not the entire story. There is considerable variation in school success among children of equivalent SES and different programs in school produce different results. But SES counts.

Study 2: Los Angeles

The Los Angeles Times (October 17, 1995) reported on transfer rates from bilingual programs in the Los Angeles Unified District. Transfer rate refers to the percentage of students who leave bilingual classes and enter mainstream classes. In the United States, this is considered an indication of success in acquiring academic English.

Transfer rates were presented according to high school cluster, which included all elementary and middle schools that fed into the high school. Twenty-seven high school clusters were listed. Within the LAUSD, transfer rates varied a great deal, from 3.1% in the cluster of schools with the lowest transfer rate to a high of 15%.

SES was not mentioned in the LA Times article. For this analysis, SES estimates were taken from LAUSD rankings, which are based on the percentage of students receiving AFDC (Aid to Families with Dependent Children) in 1992 and 1993, and the percentage of children eligible for free lunch in the same years. The scores were normalized to have a mean of 100 and a standard deviation of 17.5. The SES score for the high school (or mean of high schools when more than one was designated) was used as an estimate of the SES of the cluster.

The correlation between SES and transfer rate was positive, significant, and substantial ($r = .634$, $p < .01$, $n = 27$); clusters with higher SES ratings had higher transfer rates. SES thus accounted for 40% (r squared) of the variance in transfer rates. This is a remarkable result, considering the crudeness of the measures, and is much stronger than the effect sizes found in the Toronto data (study 1).

Inspection of the scatterplot revealed the presence of several outliers. In a post-hoc analysis, one outlier was removed (Chatsworth/Granada) and in two cases, the average transfer rate for a cluster was replaced with that of the school that was closer to the expected score. This resulted in an improved correlation of $r = .705$. The difference between this result and the original correlation was not, however, significant ($z = .438$), but the adjusted correlation produced an even more impressive r squared (49%).

Study 3: New York

There have been several articles in the press recently, reporting that children in bilingual education in New York do not exit their programs and enter the mainstream as quickly as children in all-English/ESL programs. These reports have been interpreted by critics of bilingual education as a demonstration that all-English programs are superior (e.g. Mujica, 1995).

Data from New York City confirms these reports. (New York Board of Education, 1994). Table 5.2 presents typical transfer rates.

Table 5.2.
Exit Rates and ESL/Bilingual Education Participation

EXIT AFTER THREE YEARS:

Entered at	ESL	Bilingual Ed	d	r
Kindergarten	79% (3122/3937)	42% (3161/6138)	.60	.29
Third Grade	59% (154/260)	22% (99/453)	.84	.39

from: NYC Board of Education, 1994

According to my calculations, differences in transfer rates between ESL and bilingual education students were significant (chi square = 789.57 for those entering at kindergarten, chi square = 100.84 for those entering at grade three, df = 1 in both cases). Both chi square values were easily statistically significant. Effect sizes, calculated from the chi square results, were modest.

A likely explanation for these results was presented by Luis Reyes, a member of the New York City Board of Education: "The test ... compared a group of students taking ESL courses with groups of students in the bilingual classes without controlling for external factors, like native literacy of the parents, educational level of the parents, and family income. There were a number of middle class students in the ESL program who came from countries that were more developed ... kids in the bilingual program came from where they hadn't had full schooling" (quoted in Hennelly, 1995).

A closer look at the data from NYC supports Reyes' suggestion. In NYC there was a clear relationship between first language and exit rates (table 5.3).

Table 5.3.
Exit Rates and First Language

EXIT AFTER THREE YEARS:

Entered at	Non-Spanish	Spanish	d	r
Kindergarten	75% (2855/3822)	42% (3161/6138)	.42	.21
Third Grade	50% (150/302)	21% (96/457)	.64	.31

Differences in transfer rates between non-Spanish and Spanish speaking students were statistically significant (chi square = 423.82 for kindergarten students, chi square = 68.19 for third graders, df = 1 in both cases). Note that the analysis of transfer rates according to SES and according to first language yield nearly identical results, both in terms of percentages and number of children involved. Clearly, the ESL/bilingual education comparison is also a Spanish speaker/non-Spanish speaker comparison. (The languages with the largest representation among the non-Spanish speaking population were Russian, Chinese, and Japanese.)

There is obviously nothing inherent in the Spanish language that accounts for the slower exit rate of Spanish-speaking children. More likely, Reyes is correct: Russian, Korean and Chinese speakers came from more affluent homes.

In table 5.4, I list the effect sizes (correlation coefficients) for the three studies discussed here. The Toronto and LA effect sizes indicate the impact of social class, while the New York effect sizes are based on program and first language. As noted earlier, effect sizes for the Toronto and New York studies are quite different. Note, however, that SES was measured on individual students in the Toronto study, while aggregated scores were used in the Los Angeles study: White (1982) reported that SES correlations with measures of school achievement are higher when aggregated scores are used: In 489 studies using the student as the unit of analysis, the median correlation of SES with school achievement was .221; in 93 studies using aggregated units of analysis, the median correlation of SES with school achievement was .730. Thus, the relationships reported here are quite consistent with what has been found in previous studies. Interestingly, The New York effect sizes are closer to the Toronto results, and they are also based on individual scores, which is consistent with the hypothesis that they do, in fact, reflect SES differences.

Table 5.4. Effect Sizes (correlation coefficients)		
Toronto	Born in Canada	.14
	Born outside Canada	.06
Los Angeles		.63
New York	ESL/Bilingual Ed	.29
	Non-Spanish/Spanish	.21

SES and English Language Development

Why do higher SES children appear to acquire academic English more quickly? Previous research and theory provide us with several plausible explanations, and it is likely that all of them are correct:

1. They have had more and better education in their primary language, which means more literacy and greater subject matter knowledge.

2. They have caregivers who are more educated, better prepared to help with school work in the primary language, have more time to interact with the school and more knowledge about interacting with the school (Berliner and Biddle, 1995).

3. Their greater affluence means their parents can provide tutoring in the primary language (see e.g. the case of Grace Cho, discussed in chapter two).

4. They live in a more print-rich environment, with many more books in the home (Feitelson and Goldstein, 1986; Ortiz, 1986; Raz and Bryant, 1990; Constantino, 1995; Fejgin, 1995). There is a clear relationship between living in a print-rich environment and literacy development (Ortiz,1986; Krashen, 1988; Snow, Barnes, Chandler, Goodman, and Hemphill, 1991). These children should thus have greater literacy development in the primary language, a prediction consistent with the results of studies showing a strong relationship between SES and reading achievement (So and Chan, 1983; Ortiz, 1986; Fernandez and Nielsen, 1986; Chall, Jacobs, and Baldwin, 1990; Snow et. al., 1991; Elley, 1992; Lance, Wellborn, and Hamilton-Pennell, 1993; Mullis, Campbell, and Farstrup, 1993; Krashen and O'Brian, 1996.

5. They are more likely to have access to a library. Raz and Bryant (1990) reported that middle-class children averaged more than nine trips to the library each month, while "disadvantaged" children averaged fewer than four. McQuillan (in press), in an analysis of data from the National Household Education Survey, reported that parents with higher levels of education take their children to the library more frequently.

6. They are more likely to have a quiet place to read and study at home, and are more likely to have a good diet.

SES and Bilingual Education

Well organized bilingual education programs provide, in addition to comprehensible input in English, subject matter knowledge in the primary language and literacy development in the primary language. Subject matter knowledge gained through the first language helps make the English the children hear and read more comprehensible, while literacy gained in one language transfers to the second language.

Advantages 1, 2, 3, 4 and 5, listed above, provide limited English proficient children from more affluent backgrounds with a de facto bilingual education program. Greater first language literacy, resulting from living in a more print-rich environment (advantages 4 and 5) helps children entering school at any age, while greater subject matter knowledge from previous schooling (advantage 1), parental help (advantage 2) and tutoring (advantage 3) in the primary language are of additional help to those entering later than kindergarten.

Implied in the above discussion is the view that SES is not causative. Rather, factors typically associated with high SES are causative. The presence of reading materials in the home is associated with social class, but contributes to reading achievement independent of the contribution of social class (Ortiz, 1986; Fejgin, 1995). Thus, high SES is not the only way to provide these advantages. Low SES children have succeeded, as several scholars have pointed out (Cummins, 1984) (and some high SES children have not). What is crucial is that we can improve the achievement of LEP children by providing these factors in school.

The interpretation of the Toronto, LA and NY data presented here, if correct, is both good news and bad news. It confirms that our bilingual programs are on the right track when they provide literacy and subject matter knowledge in the primary language. In doing this, they replicate those aspects of the high SES child's home environment that are helpful for school. But finding a strong positive relationship between SES and school success tells us that we have not yet managed to level the playing field: Our goal should be programs in which SES is not predictive of English language development, schools that provide such a rich print environment, and such excellent education in the primary language that outside factors do not matter.

References

Berliner, D. and Biddle, D. 1995. The Manufactured Crisis. Reading, MA: Addison-Wesley,

Chall, J., Jacobs, V., and Baldwin, L. 1990. The Reading Crises: Why Poor Children Fall Behind. Cambridge: Harvard University Press.

Constantino, R. 1995. Two small girls, one big disparity. The Reading Teacher 48: 504.

Cummins, J. 1984. Bilingualism and Special Education: Issues in Assessment and Pedagogy. Clevedon, England: Multilingual Matters.

Elley, W. 1992. How in the World do Students Read? Hamburg: International Association for the Evaluation of Educational Achievement.

Feitelson, D. and Goldstein, Z. 1986. Patterns of book ownership and reading to young children in Israeli school-oriented and nonschool oriented families. The Reading Teacher 39: 924-230.

Fajgin, N. 1995. Factors contributing to the academic excellence of American Jewish and Asian students. Sociology of Education 68: 18-30.

Fernandez, R. and Nielson, F. 1986. Bilingualism and Hispanic scholastic achievement: Some baseline results. Social Science Research 15: 43-70.

Hennelly, R. 1995. NYC bilingual study clarified. Multicultural Newsletter, Peoples Publishing Group, International Multicultural Education Association, Maywood, NJ. 2,2:1-2.

Johnson, B. 1989. DSTAT: Software for the Meta-Analytic Review of Research Literature. Hillsdale, NJ: Erlbaum.

Krashen, S. 1988. Do we learn to read by reading? The relationship between free reading and reading ability. In D. Tannen (Ed.) Linguistics in Context: Connecting Observation and Understanding. Norwood, NJ: Ablex. pp. 269-298.

Krashen, S. and O'Brian, B. 1996. School library collections and reading achievement in Los Angeles and Beyond. Indiana Media Journal 18,3: 71-77.

Lance, K., Welborn, L., and Hamilton-Pennell, C. 1993.The Impact of School Library Media Centers on Academic Achievement. Englewood, Colorado: Libraries Unlimited.

McArthur, 1993. Language Characteristics and Schooling in the United States, A Changing Picture: 1979 and 1989. Washington: US Govemment Printing Office.

McQuillan, J. (in press) Language minority students and public library use in the United States.

Mujica, B. 1995. Findings of the New York City longitudinal study: Hard evidence on bilingual and ESL programs. READ Perspectives 2,2:7-34.

Mullis, I., Campbell, J. and Farstrup, A. 1993. NAEP 1992: Reading Report Card for the Nation and the States. Washington, DC: US Department of Education.

New York City Board of Education. 1994. Educational Progress of Students in Bilingual and ESL Programs: A Longitudinal Study, 1990-1994. NYC Board of Education.

Ortiz, V. 1986. Reading activities and reading proficiency among Hispanic, Black, and White students. American Journal of Education 95: 58-76.

Raz, I. and Bryant, P. 1990. Social background, phonological awareness and children's reading. British Journal of Developmental Psychology 8: 209-225.

Rosenthal, A., Milne, A. Ellman, F., Ginsburg, A. and Baker, K. 1983. A comparison of the effects of language background and socioeconomic status on achievement among elementary-school students. In Baker, K. and de Kanter, E. (Eds.) Bilingual Education: A Reappraisal of Federal Policy. Lexington, MA: Lexington Books. pp. 87-111.

Snow, C., Barnes, W., Chandler, J., Goodman, 1., and Hemphill, L. 1991. Unfulfilled Expectations: Home and School Influences on Literacy. Cambridge: Harvard University Press.

So, A. and Chan, K. 1983. What matters? The relative impact of language background and socioeconomic status on reading achievement. NABE Journal 7: 27-41.

White, K. 1982. The relation between socioeconomic status and academic achievement. Psychological Bulletin 91: 461-481.

Chapter Six:
Is the Public Against Bilingual Education?

Opponents of bilingual education tell us that surveys show that the public is against bilingual education. This impression is a result of the way the question has been asked. One can easily get a near 100% rejection of bilingual education when the question is biased. Porter (1991), for example, states that "Many parents are not committed to having the schools maintain the mother tongue if it is at the expense of gaining a sound education and the English-language skills needed for obtaining jobs or pursuing higher education" (p. 8).

I don't know anyone who would support primary language education at such a price–I would not.

Similarly, Chavez (1991) reports that:

"A study by the Educational Testing Service ... found that the overwhelming majority of Hispanic parents - 78 percent of Mexican Americans and 82 percent of the Cubans - opposed teaching the child's native language if it meant less time for teaching English" (p. 29).

Stated in this way, with the clear implication that less time for teaching English means less English language development, very few people would support bilingual education. The question presupposes that bilingual education is not good for English and is misleading, because an important and central goal of bilingual education is to promote English language development, and well-organized programs do this effectively.

Consider also this statement: "I want my children in an all-English class so that they can learn English faster." In Snipper (1986), Hispanic parents showed strong agreement with this statement (3.8 out of a possible 5, where 5 = strongly agree, 1 = strongly disagree). This is not surprising, because the statement presupposes that children will learn English faster in an all-English class.

Do You Support Bilingual Education?

When respondants are simply asked whether they support bilingual education, the degree of support is much greater (table 6.1).

Table 6.1.a
Support for Bilingual Education: Global

Torres, 1988: *Support for "Home language as a teaching tool" (table 5)*

1. Parents on Bilingual School
   Advisory Committee (n = 41)   Strongly agree or agree = **95.1%**

2. Parents not on committee, but with   Strongly agree or agree = **99%**
   children in bilingual education (n = 106)

3. School principals (n = 11)   Strongly agree or agree = **100%**

Youssef and Simpkins, 1985: *44 parents of children in Arabic bilingual program*

"I am pleased that my child is in a bilingual   Strongly agree + agree = **97%**
  program." (question 1)

"Bilingual education should not be a part of   Strongly disagree + disagree = **55%**
  the school curriculum" (question 19)

"Do you want your child to attend bilingual   yes = **95%**
  classes?" (question 27)

Attinasi, 1985: *65 Latinos living in Northern Indiana.*

"Want children in bilingual education"   yes = **89%**

Aguirre, 1984: *600 parents of children in bilingual programs, 60 bilingual teachers*

"Bilingual education is acceptable in the
  school because it is the best means
  for meeting theeducational needs of the   Agree: Parents = **80%**
  limited English proficient child." (question F)   Teachers = **90%**

Hosch, 1984: *Survey of 283 subjects, from random voter lists, El Paso County, Texas.*

"Last year, the state of Texas spent $31.00 per
  student enrolled in bilingual education
  programs. Do you think this should be
  eliminated/decreased by 1/4/maintained   Support for maintained
  /increased by 2X/increased 4X?" (question 19).   or increased funding = **64.3%**

Table 6.1.b
Support for Bilingual Education: Global (continued)

Shin and Kim, *in press: 56 Korean parents with children in elementary school*

Would place child in bilingual classroom
  where both Korean and English are used
  as a medium of instruction.   Yes = **70%**

Shin and Lee, *1996: Hmong parents with children in elementary school*

Would place child in bilingual classroom
  where both Hmong and English are used
  as a medium of instruction.   Yes = **60%**

The questions in table 6.1 probe global support for bilingual education in a variety of ways, with a variety of groups, in a variety of places. No matter how the question is asked, however, most respondants support bilingual education. This contrasts with responses to loaded questions that assume that promoting the primary language is bad for English.

Support for the Underlying Principles

In a series of studies, Shin (Shin and Kim, in press; Shin and Gribbons, in press; Shin and Krashen, forthcoming; Shin and Lee, 1996; Lee and Shin, 1996) examined attitudes toward the principles underlying bilingual education. Her results are presented in table 6.2. What is clear from inspection of her data is that there is considerable support for the principles underlying bilingual education. Specifically, Shin found that:

- a substantial number of respondees agree with the idea that the first language can be helpful in providing background knowledge;

- most agree with the argument that literacy transfers across languages;

- most support the principles underlying continuing bilingual education.

This data confirms that there is considerable support for bilingual education.

The number of people opposed to bilingual education is probably even less than the responses to these questions suggest. Many people who say they are opposed to bilingual education are, in reality, not opposed to the idea of bilingual education, but are opposed to certain practices or are opposed to regulations connected to bilingual education.

Table 6.2.
Attitudes Toward the Principles Underlying Bilingual Education

	Korean parents	Hispanic parents	Hmong parents	Teachers
Rationale for advantages of early bilingual education				
1. Learning subject matter through the first language helps make subject matter study in English more comprehensible	47%	34%[a]	60%	70%
2. Developing literacy in the first language facilitates literacy development in English	88%	53%[b]	52%	74%
Rationale for advantages of continuing bilingual education				
1. Practical, career-related advantages	97%	75%	86%	85%
2. Superior cognitive development	86%	61%	89%	71%

a: *33% of the sample were "not sure."*
b: *21% were "not sure"*

Korean parents: Shin and Kim, in press.	n = 256
Hispanic parents: Shin and Gribbons, 1996.	n = 150
Hmong parents: Shin and Lee, 1996; Lee and Shin, 1996.	n = 100
Teachers: Shin and Krashen, 1996.	n = 794

One such practice is the misplacement of children.

Misplacement

There have been two "misplacement" arguments. The first involves the placement in bilingual education classes of children who speak English very well, and who, in some cases, do not speak the other language. Chavez (1991), for example, notes that one of her children was placed in a bilingual program simply on the basis of the fact that his first name was "Pablo" and his mother's name was Chavez: "They did not bother to ascertain that English was his first and only language" (p. 30).

This is, of course, bad policy. The presence of such incompetence has nothing to do, however, with whether bilingual education is justified.

Other cases of "misplacement" involve children who can speak some English. Chavez (1991) attributes this opinion to Sally Peterson, founder of Learning English Advocates Drive: "One of Peterson's chief compaints regards student placement: She maintains that Hispanic students who have enough English to benefit from an all-English instructional program, particularly a structured English-immersion approach that compensates for the child's limited vocabulary, are being put into Spanish-language classrooms" (p. 34). Chavez' own observations agree with Peterson's. In her visits to bilingual programs, she notes that:

" ... I have witnessed Mexican, Salvadoran, Guatemalan, and other Hispanic children being taught grammar, reading, math, and social science lessons in Spanish, yet nearly all the students exhibited some command of English. In several classrooms, I observed very young Hispanic children working together at their tables speaking English among themselves as their teachers gave directions in Spanish. In some bilingual schools, I watched Hispanic children as young as six or seven years old conversing freely in English as they lined up for lunch or playground. Left to choose their language, they spoke exclusively in English–even when no Anglo students were within earshot. Clearly, such children do not need to be taught in Spanish ..." (p. 37).

(See also Porter, 1991, pp. 21-22, 66-67 for similar observations.)

The issue here is whether these children have enough English to do all subjects in the mainstream or in sheltered classes. If they do, Peterson and Chavez are of course correct, and they should not be in bilingual education programs. (They will probably benefit a great deal, however, from continued first language development; see e.g. Krashen and Biber, 1988).

Most likely, some of these children, despite conversational fluency, lack "academic language" (Cummins, 1981) and would fit into the intermediate or advanced levels of a bilingual program, with enough English to do some subjects in English, but not all. They may not have enough academic English competence to do subjects such as social studies and language arts in English, and would profit from first language instruction in these areas. Just because a child has some English competence does not mean he or she is ready to do the entire program in English.

Again, questions of placement are simply that, questions of placement. They are legitimate questions and deserve investigation. They cannot be considered as valid criticisms of the concept of bilingual education, only as complaints about how particular programs are run.

Need Teachers Acquire the Child's Language?

A second source of opposition to bilingual education is the policy that some districts have of insisting that monolingual teachers acquire the child's language, because of the shortage of qualified bilingual teachers. I have, of course, nothing against non-bilinguals attempting to acquire the child's first language. In fact, I think it is an excellent idea. It helps give teachers real insight into the language acquisition process, allows them to help out in the primary language when needed, and helps them communicate with parents.

But high level mastery of the child's language should not be a prerequisite to teaching in a bilingual program. In fact, insistence that teachers acquire the child's first language has been a serious obstacle to the acceptance of bilingual education. To acquire a second language to a level high enough to teach in it, to acquire "academic" knowledge of a language, takes much more time and energy than most teachers have. Certainly, Natural Approach and sheltered subject matter classes will help, but this will only bring acquirers to the intermediate level, which is all the classroom can do.

To be truly comfortable and effective teaching in Spanish, for example, I recommend extensive pleasure reading, extensive academic reading, and extensive interaction with native speakers in a variety of situations. While not necessary, the most practical way of doing this is to spend several years in a Spanish-speaking country, working in Spanish, socializing in Spanish, and interacting a great deal with Spanish-speaking children. The solutions to the teacher shortage in bilingual education must come from other sources, such as team-teaching, education of para-professionals, and promoting heritage language programs. Insisting that overworked monolingual teachers acquire the child's language to high levels of competence only inspires opposition to bilingual education for the wrong reasons.

Unreasonable demands on teachers need to be stopped. They do not, however, invalidate the underlying principles of bilingual education, and they do not imply that bilingual education is a bad idea. If there were a shortage of algebra teachers, and if non-math teachers were suddenly forced to learn and teach algebra, we would not vote to drop algebra. Instead, we would look for more reasonable ways to find algebra teachers.

It is a reasonable assumption that many who object to bilingual education on the grounds of misapplication would support it if application were improved. Some might not, however: Another group of objectors are those who are opposed to our schools providing education in the child's primary language, even if it is beneficial. Within this group, there may be several subgroups: Those who sincerely object to the use of languages other than English on patriotic grounds, those who feel that immigrants present some kind of economic threat, and those with xenophobic and racist points of view.

Summary and Conclusion

If you ask people if they support the development of the first language at the expense of English and school success, nearly all will say "no." But if you ask them if they support bilingual education, a surprising number say they do. Similarly, a large percentage agree with the principles underlying bilingual education. When people do object to bilingual education, quite often it is on the basis of application, not theory.

Such support is amazing, when we consider what the public reads about bilingual education. McQuillan and Tse (1996) reviewed publications appearing between 1984 and 1994, and reported that 87% of academic publications supported bilingual education, but newspaper and magazine opinion articles tended to be anti-bilingual education, with only 45% supporting bilingual education. When the non-professional tries to find out about bilingual education from the local bookstore, the picture is similar: Attacks on bilingual education, such as Porter's *Forked Tongue*, and Chavez' *Out of the Barrio*, are easy to find. Explanations and defenses of bilingual education, such as Crawford's *Hold Your Tongue* and Berliner and Biddle's *The Manufactured Crisis* are much harder to find. Most obvious are the many attacks on bilingual education from organizations such as US English, as advertisements in national magazines. One wonders what support would look like if bilingual education were presented in a more positive light.

References

Aguirre, A. 1984. Parent and teacher opinions of bilingual education: Comparisons and contrasts. NABE Journal 9 (1): 41-51.

Attinasi, J. 1985. Hispanic attitudes in Northwest Indiana and New York. In L. Elias-Olivares, E. Leone, R. Cisneros, and J. Gutierrez (Eds.) Spanish Language Use and Public Life in the United States. New York: Mouton. pp. 28-58.

Berliner, D. and Biddle, D. 1995. The Manufactured Crisis. Reading, MA: Addison-Wesley,

Chavez, L. 1991. Out of the Barrio. New York: Basic Books.

Crawford, J. 1992. Hold Your Tongue. Reading, MA: Addison-Wesley.

Cummins, J. 1981. The role of primary language development in promoting educational success for language minority students. In Schooling and Language Minority Students. Sacramento, CA: California Department of Education. pp. 3-49.

Hosch, H. 1984. Attitudes Toward Bilingual Education: A View from the Border. University of Texas, El Paso: Texas Western Press.

Krashen, S. and Biber, D. 1988. On Course: Bilingual Education's Success in California. Ontario, CA: California Association for Bilingual Education.

Lee, B. and Shin, F. 1996. Hmong parents' perceptions of bilingual education. CAAPAE Newsletter (California Association of Asian Pacific American Education), Spring, 1996, 7-8.

McQuillan, J. and Tse, L. 1996.Does research really matter? An analysis of media opinion on bilingual education, 1984-1994. Bilingual Research Journal 20(1): 1-27.

Porter, R. 1991. Forked Tongue. New York: Basic Books.

Shin, F. and Lee, B. 1996. Hmong parents and students: What do they think about bilingual education? Pacific Educational Research Journal 8(1): 65-71.

Shin, F. 1994. Attitudes of Korean parents toward bilingual education. BEOutreach Newsletter, California State Department of Education, 5(2): 47-48.

Shin, F. and Kim, S. Korean parent perceptions and attitudes of bilingual education. In R. Endo, C. Park, J. Tsuchida, and A. Agbayani (Eds.) Current Issues in Asian and Pacific American Education. Covina, CA: Pacific Asian Press. In press.

Shin, F. and Gribbons, B. 1996. Hispanic parent perceptions and attitudes of bilingual education. The Journal of Mexican-American Educators. pp. 16-22

Shin, F. and Krashen, S. 1996. Teachers' attitudes toward the principles of bilingual education and toward students' participation in bilingual programs: Same or different? Bilingual Research Journal 20(1): 45-53.

Snipper, G. 1986. Real Americans don't speak Spanish: Some Hispanic parents' views of bilingual education. Bilingual Review 13: 171-185.

Torres, M. 1988. Attitudes of bilingual education parents toward language learning and curriculum instruction. NABE Journal 12 (2):171-185.

Youssef, A. and Simpkins, E. 1985. Parent attitudes on Americanization and bilingual education: The Dearborn, Detroit, and Farmington study. Bilingual Review 12:190-197.

Chapter Seven: Is English in Trouble?

The impression we get from the media is that immigrants today are not acquiring English; in fact it is sometimes claimed that they resist it.

Beard-Williams (1994), in an Op-Ed article in the Los Angeles Times, asserts, "At what point do we hold non-English-speaking persons accountable for their disinterest (sic) in learning the language of this country ...". Turbak (1994), in Reader's Digest, writes about "the erosion of English" (p. 178) and claims that "LEP children often remain in native-language classes for several years, and some never learn English" (p. 178).

Reports such as these motivate proposals to protect the English language in the United States, including the proposal to make English our official language. In reality, immigrants, both children and adults, are not at all reluctant to use English, and are doing an incredible job of acquiring it. In fact, it is the home languages that are eroding.

I present here a brief survey of a very consistent body of research that shows that non-native speakers of English who live in the US use English a great deal and have acquired it remarkably well. Acquisition of conversational English, however, does not necessarily entail the acquisition of academic English (Cummins, 1989), and school can do a great deal to ensure the development of academic English.

Studies of Language Use

Many studies have confirmed the presence of intergenerational shift, the finding that English language use is much more common among children than among parents, and that first language use is much more common among parents than children. Table 7.1 presents a series of studies documenting this shift. Among the significant results of the studies are these:

- Hispanics who are members of the younger generation report far more use of English, and less use of Spanish, than their parents (Laosa, 1975; Skrabanek,

1970), and those born in the US use English more than they use Spanish (Lopez, 1978; Veltman, 1983).

- Analyses of data from the US Census shows that about 50% of those with Spanish as a first language report more use of English as their language of communication (Veltman, 1983; Grenier, 1984).

- English is very strong among high school students (Sole, 1982; Veltman, 1983; Garcia and Diaz, 1992; Hakuta and d'Andrea, 1992), and is evident even among very young children (Laosa, 1984).

Table 7.1
Studies of Language Use

Skrabanek (1970): *Mexican-Americans Rural Texas*

LANGUAGE USED SOCIALLY

Generation	Mostly Spanish	Equal	Mostly English
Adults	68%	26%	6%
Ages 18-24	44%	42%	14%
Ages 10-17	31%	45%	24%

(adults: 268 households; 18-24: 80 households; 10-17: 145 households)

Skrabanek (1970): *Mexican Americans San Antonio*

LANGUAGE USED SOCIALLY

Generation	Mostly Spanish	Equal	Mostly English
Adults	58%	33%	9%
Ages 18-24	25%	39%	36%
Ages 10-17	17%	37%	46%

(adults: 276 households; 18-24: 43 households; 10-17: 128 households)

Laosa (1975): *Mexican-Americans (Austin), most born in US, 100 families*

LANGUAGE USED INFORMALLY

Generation	English	Spanish
Adults	26%	23%
Children (grades 1-3)	89%	1%

(does not include subjects who used both or mixture)

Laosa (1975): *Cuban-Americans, most born in Cuba, 100 families*

LANGUAGE USED INFORMALLY

Generation	English	Spanish
Adults	9%	84%
Children (grades 1-3)	26%	40%

(does not include subjects who used both or mixture)

Table 7.1
Studies of Language Use (continued)

Lopez (1978): Married Chicano women in LA

CURRENT USE OF SPANISH

Generation	n	Spanish	Both	English
First	493	84%	14%	2%
Second	158	15%	19%	66%
Third	239	4%	12%	84%

(First: born and riased in Mexico; second: born and raised in US, parents born and raised in Mexico; third: parents born in US)

Sole 1982: 268 Cuban-American high school students, ages 14-18, 80% born in Cuba, most came to US before age ten

LANGUAGE PREFERENCE

English	25%
Both	42%

"The entire sample claimed to have acquired English" (p. 260).

Veltman (1983): 1976 Survey of Income and Education, 158,000 households, ages 4-17

Parental language	Percent English usual language
Navajo	17.3%
Spanish	52.4%
Other	53.4%

Veltman (1983): 1976 Survey of Income and Education, ages 14 and older

ENGLISH AS USUAL LANGUAGE

Home language	Foreign Born	US born
Spanish	29%	65%
Other	64%	94%

Veltman (1983): High School Students

Home language	n	Home language used with friends
Spanish	3594	1.63
Other	1154	.89

(0 = Never; 1 = Sometimes; 2 = About half the time; 3 = Mostly; 4 = Always)

Table 7.1
Studies of Language Use (continued)

Grenier (1984): *n = 7,366, "People of Spanish mother tongue"*
USE OF SPANISH AS MAIN LANGUAGE OF COMMUNICATION

Mexican American	48%
Puerto-Rican	57%
Cuban-American	68%
All groups	50%

Laosa (1984): *84 Chicano families (San Antonio), most born in USA*

Mother speaks to child in English	64.4%
Child speaks English to mother	74.4%
Father speaks to child in English	62.7%
Child speaks to father in English	74.2%

(Mean age of children = 2 years, 6 months)

Wong Fillmore (1991): *Children in all English or bilingual programs, 690 families*
PERCENT USING ENGLISH ONLY OR MOSTLY

	With Adults	*With Siblings*
Older Children	31%	40%
Middle	30.5%	41%
Young	27%	34%

Gersten, Woodward, and Schneider (1992): *59 Sixth graders in bilingual programs (El Paso)*

Which language do you feel most comfortable speaking in?
"Almost a third...felt more comfortable speaking Spanish" (p.26)
Two-thirds prefer English or have no preference.

Garcia and Diaz (1992): *394 Cuban-American high school seniors (Florida)*
LANGUAGE USED: SPANISH OR SPANISH WITH SOME ENGLISH

Preschool	85%
Junior high school	37%
Senior high school	18%

Pease-Alvarez and Winsler (1994): *3 fourth graders in bilingual education; teacher speaks English, some Spanish*

English use in School	*Beginning of School Year*	*End of School Year*
Sebastian	90%	100%
Raul	80%	92%
Christina	30%	40%

Table 7.1
Studies of Language Use (continued)

Hakuta and d'Andrea (1992): 308 Mexican-American high school students

LANGUAGE USED WITH PEERS (1 = SPANISH; 5 = ENGLISH)

Arrived in USA after age 10	2.1
Arrived in USA between 6-10	2.8
Arrived in USA age 5 or younger	3.2
Born in USA, both parents born in Mexico	3.7
Born in USA, one parent born in USA	4.3
Born in USA, one parent, grandparent born in USA	4.2

Studies of Language Proficiency

Language use may or may not be an accurate reflection of proficiency. As Pedraza and Pousada (1992) point out, a speaker "may be forced out of circumstances to use a language other than the one he manipulates best" (p. 257). In their study, the relationship between language use and proficiency was positive, but not perfect (see also Veltman, 1983).

In several studies, actual proficiency is examined. Despite differences in methodology, year the study was published, and location, the results are similar and converge with the results of language use studies. The results (table 7.2) include the following:

- A surprising number of Mexican-American children appear to be English dominant for conversational language at a young age (Carrow, 1971).

- More members of the younger generation report high proficiency in English than in Spanish; for the older generation, more report high proficiency in Spanish (Hudson-Edwards and Bills, 1980).

- As children grow up, they become more English dominant (Merino, 1983; Veltman, 1983), even in heavily Spanish-speaking areas (McConnell, 1985).

- Spanish ability remains fairly high among high school seniors in Florida, but their English ability is also high, and students rank themselves more highly in English writing than Spanish writing (Garcia and Diaz, 1992).

- For those born in the US, the shift to English is typically complete by high school, and even for those who immigrate, English is often strong at this age (Veltman, 1983; Tse 1996[1]).

- The number of English-only speakers among Navajos increased significantly

Table 7.2a.
Proficiency (Tested)

Carrow (1971): *99 Mexican-American children, ages 3 to 9, low SES, Houston, Texas*

SCORES ON TEST OF AURAL COMPREHENSION

Age	English	Spanish
3-10 to 4-3	65	56
4-4 to 4-9	72	46
4-10 to 5-3	79	62
5-4 to 5-9	78	68
5-10 to 6-9	95	67

(Similar items tested in English and Spanish versions, weaker language tested first.)

Merino (1983): *32 children, K-4, all "balanced bilinguals" at age five*

Category	Time 1	Time 2 (2 years later)
Spanish production (BLAS)		
Past Tense	87%	74%
Relatives	100%	44%
Subjunctive	70%	55%
English Production		
Word Order	42%	93%
Relatives	66%	85%
Conditionals	53%	84%

McConnell (1985): *Children ages 5-8, Texas (Heavy Spanish-speaking area)*

PERCENTAGE OF CHILDREN DOMINANT IN ENGLISH
(High English scores than Spanish scores on Peabody vocabulary test)

Years in bilingual program	Percent
1	2%
2	7%
3	28%

Children ages 5-8, Washington State (Heavy English-speaking area)

PERCENTAGE OF CHILDREN DOMINANT IN ENGLISH

Years in bilingual program	Percent
1	33%
2	60%
3	70%

Total n (both studies) = approx. 700

Table 7.2b.
Proficiency (Self-Reported)

Hudson-Edwards and Bills (1980): *Mexican-Americans in Albuquerque (Martineztown, Spanish-speaking community)*

NUMBER CLAIMING "GOOD" OR "VERY GOOD" ABILITY

Generation	Spanish Ability	English Ability
Junior	33% (26/80)	81% (69-81)
Senior	85% (74/87)	47% (41/88)

(Senior: Heads of households, spouces, siblings; junior; children of heads)

Veltman (1983): *High school students*

Home Language	n	Self-rating of reading		Writing	
		First Language	English	First Language	English
Spanish	3594	1.94	2.57	1.71	2.51
Other	1154	1.56	2.62	1.37	2.55

(0 = Not at all, 1 = Not very well, 2 = Pretty well, 3 = Very well)

McCarthy and Valdez (1985): *Mexican-Americans*

Percent describing themselves as monolingual English

Second Generation	50%
First Generation	Over 25%

Garcia and Diaz (1992): *394 Cuban-American high school seniors, Dade County, Florida*

	Spanish	English
Understand	90%	85%
Speak	87%	78%
Read	79%	75%
Write	66%	80%

Tse (1996): *High school students*

Subjects: First Language	Self-rating of reading		Writing	
	In First Language	In English	In First Language	In English
Asian	3.1	3.0	2.8	2.8
Spanish born in US	3.6	3.8	3.2	3.8
Spanish foreign born	3.9	3.1	3.8	3.1

(1 = Not at all 4 = Very well)
Sample size: Asian, tested in first language = 62; Asian, tested in English = 59; Spanish, (born in US) = 16; Spanish (foreign born) = 19

Table 7.2b.
Proficiency (continued)

Crawford (1995): Navajo speakers

Percent who speak only English
1980   7%
1990   15%

Bills, Hernandex-Chavez, and Hudson (1995): *1980 Census for 22 cities (samples presented here)*

PERCENT OF "SPANISH ORIGIN" CLAIMING SPANISH AS HOME LANGUAGE

City	Adults	Youth (ages 5-17)
El Paso	97	93
Los Angeles	92	83
Sacramento	80	69
Denver	56	31

Table 7.2c.
Proficiency (Parent Evaluation)

Wong-Fillmore (1991): *Children in all-English or bilingual programs, 690 families*

SPEAKS L1 POORLY OR INADQUATELY FOR AGE

Older children	35%
Middle	42%
Young	43%

over a ten year period; the increase was most marked in the age 5 to 17 group, with English-only speakers increasing from 12 to 28% (Crawford, 1995).

- Fewer young people of Hispanic origin report Spanish to be their home language (Bills, Hernandez-Chavez, and Hudson, 1995).[2]

Misreporting the Facts

Misreporting the facts has contributed to the impression that immigrants are not acquiring English. McArthur (1993) reports statistics from the US Census on English language development of people ages five and older in 1979 and 1989. According to her analysis of the data, "Almost half of the Spanish speakers ... reported speaking English with difficulty in 1989 ..." (p. iii), a conclusion that certainly supports public opinion.

Krashen and McQuillan (1995) reanalyzed McArthur's data and came to very different conclusions. In the census, respondents were asked to rate their English on a four-point scale: "very well", "well", "not well", and "not at all." Strangely, McArthur, in summarizing the data, categorized all those who reported that they spoke English "well," "not well", and "not at all" as having difficulty with English. In other words those who said they spoke English well were classified as having difficulty! Consider the 1989 results for native speakers of Spanish:

I speak English:

Very well	50.5%
Well	21.0%
Not well	19.7%
Not at all	8.8%

According to McArthur's categorization, it is indeed true that almost half have difficulty with English. But if we include those who say they speak English "well" as not having difficulty, we can conclude that over 70% do not have difficulty with English, and fewer than 9% don't speak English at all. This is very impressive, considering that the figures undoubtedly include new arrivals.

Hispanics are usually portrayed as the most reluctant to acquire English. McArthur's report says otherwise. There was no difference at all between Spanish speakers and speakers of Asian/Pacific Island languages in self-report of English competence:

I speak English:

First Language	"very well or well"	"not at all"
Spanish	71.5%	8.8%
Asian/Pacific Isl.	72.3%	7.6%

The impression some people have that Spanish speakers are not acquiring English is due to the presence of new immigrants and visitors. But even they have done remarkably well in acquiring English. McCarthey and Valdez (1985) reported that among Mexican-Americans born in the US, more than 90% said they were proficient in English (see also Veltman, 1983). Among the foreign born who are permanent residents of the US, over 75% said they spoke some English and nearly half said they spoke English well. About 25% of short-term and cyclical visitors said they spoke English well and over half reported some competence in English. McCarthy and Valdez concluded that "the transition to English begins almost immediately and proceeds very rapidly" (p. 28).

Do We Need Special Programs?

If English is acquired by immigrants, do we need special programs? To see how special programs can help, we first need to consider the conversational-academic language distinction.

Conversational versus academic language

Cummins (1989) makes the important distinction between "conversational" and "academic" language. Conversational language is the language of everyday interaction. It is heavily "contextualized," that is, aspects of the situation help make input comprehensible and reduce the necessity of adding information for the speaker. "Academic" language is the language of school, politics, science, and business, and is more "decontextualized," that is, it must be comprehended with less contextual help.

Studies showing acquisition of English and intergenerational shift typically deal with conversational language, not academic language: Children rapidly pick up conversational language, but this does not automatically mean the acquisition of academic language. In their study of 100 Latino high school students designated as being "at risk" of dropping out of school, Romo and Falbo (1996) reported that "almost all the students in our sample were comfortable speaking in English ... yet, almost all students in our sample experienced a skills deficit in reading" (p. 9); although the students were in the seventh to eleventh grades, their average reading score was sixth-grade. In other words, they had conversational English, but not academic English.

Why ESL

It is true that given enough exposure to language in the informal environment, acquisition of conversational language will take place. ESL classes can make the process easier, quicker, and less painful. According to current theory (Krashen, 1994), we acquire language when we get comprehensible input, messages we understand. The "outside world" will not always provide comprehensible input; for the beginner, it may be weeks until even simple messages are comprehensible. In a well-taught language class, however, a beginner can get 40 minutes of comprehensible input the first day. ESL classes can be very efficient for beginners.

Beyond ESL

ESL is very helpful, but it is limited to conversational language. For most people, however, conversational language is not enough. There are several ways of developing academic language, and all of them can be used at the same time.

The first is free voluntary reading (Krashen, 1993). It has been established that free reading, reading we do because we want to, is the major source of our reading ability, our vocabulary knowledge, our spelling ability, vocabulary size, and ability to deal with complex grammatical constructions. Richard Rodriguez developed conversational language from interaction, but developed academic language by becoming a voracious reader. In *Hunger of Memory*, he reports, "I entered high school having read hundreds of books. My habit of reading made me a confident speaker and writer of English." (Rodriguez, 1982, p. 63).

Suggesting free reading is easy, but limited English proficient children may have a hard time doing it, because of lack of access to books (Pucci, 1994). Developing and giving children access to high quality school libraries, doing sustained silent reading, and developing a taste for reading through literature classes are means of overcoming this problem.

A second way is to participate in "sheltered" subject matter classes, academic classes taught in English that are made comprehensible for the second language acquirer. Participants in these classes acquire a great deal of academic language as well as subject matter knowledge (Krashen, 1991).

A third way is the proper use of the child's first language. Instruction delivered in the primary language can have a profound effect on the development of academic English. First, the primary language can be used to teach subject matter - if children know subject matter, they will understand much more of what goes on in classes taught in English, resulting in more language acquisition as well as knowledge. Second, the primary language can be used to develop literacy, which transfers to the second language. There is evidence that programs that utilize the first language in this way are effective in promoting academic English language development (Krashen and Biber, 1988).

Thus, the fact that immigrants typically do acquire conversational English does not mean that educational efforts are useless (see also Waggoner, 1989). ESL classes can facilitate the development of conversational language, and efforts to promote free reading, sheltered subject matter teaching, and properly designed bilingual programs can help in the development of academic language.

Finally, it needs to be said that the loss of the first language is not necessary, and is not a good thing. Developing the first language does not harm English language development. In fact, as long as English language development occurs, continued first language development is related to superior scholastic achievement (Nielsen and Lerner, 1986; Fernandez and Nielsen, 1986) with no socioeconomic disadvantages (Tienda and Neidert, 1984).

Notes

1. Note that in Tse's studies, foreign born Spanish speakers reported very high competence in their primary language. These students were, however, enrolled in classes in Spanish for native speakers of Spanish.

2. Additional evidence confirming that children become quite competent in English at a surprisingly fast rate is their reported ability to act as interpreters for parents and others in a short time. Tse (1996) studied 64 high school students who acquired English as a second language, and who spoke either Chinese or Vietnamese as a first language. Nearly 90% said they had "brokered"; 52% said they began brokering within one year after their arrival in the United States, and 62% began within two years (ten subjects did not indicate the age at which they started brokering and two were born in the United States).

Tse (1995) did a similar study of Spanish speakers currently in high school. 56% of her United States-born subjects began brokering by age ten, and all brokered by age 14. Among those born abroad, 13% brokered within two years, 38% within four years and 88% within five years.

Finally, McQuillan and Tse (1995), in their study of nine subjects, ages 18 to 29, reported that brokering began soon after arrival in the US.

References

Beard-Williams, D. 1994. We speak English in L.A.; Don't apologize. Los Angeles Times, December 1, 1994.

Bills, G., Hernandez Chavez, E., and Hudson, A. 1995. The geography of language shift: Distance from the Mexican border and Spanish language claiming in the Southwestern US. International Journal of the Sociology of Language 114: 9-27.

Carrow, E. 1971. Comprehension of English and Spanish by preschool Mexican-American children. Modern Language Journal 55: 299-306.

Crawford, J. 1995. Endangered Native American languages: What is to be done, and why? Bilingual Research Journal 19:17-38.

Cummins, J. 1989. Empowering Minority Students. Ontario, CA: California Association for Bilingual Education.

Fernandez, R. and Nielsen, F. 1986. Bilingualism and Hispanic scholastic achievement: some baseline results. Social Science Research 15: 43-70.

Garcia, R. and Diaz, C. 1992. The status and use of Spanish and English among Hispanic youth in Dade County (Miami) Florida: A sociolinguistic study. Language and Education 6: 13-32.

Gersten, R., Woodward, J., and Schneider, S. 1992. Bilingual Immersion: A Longitudinal Evaluation of the El Paso Program. Washington, DC: The Read Institute.

Grenier, G. 1984. Shifts to English as usual language by Americans of Spanish mother tongue. Social Science Quarterly 65: 537-550.

Hakuta, K. and D'Andrea, D. 1992. Some properties of bilingual maintenance and loss in Mexican background high-school students. Applied Linguistics 13: 72-99.

Hudson-Edwards, A., and Bills, G. 1980. International language shift in an Albuquerque barrio. In E. Blansitt and R. Teschner (Eds.) A Festschrift for Jacob Ornstein. New York: Newbury House. pp.139-158.

Krashen, S. 1991. Sheltered subject matter teaching. Cross Currents 18:183-189.

Krashen, S. 1994. The input hypothesis and its rivals. In N. Ellis (Ed.) Implicit and Explicit Learning of Languages. London: Academic Press. pp. 45-77.

Krashen, S. and Biber, D. 1988. On Course: Bilingual Education's Success in California. Ontario: California Association for Bilingual Education.

Krashen, S. and McQuillan, J. 1995. Contrary to popular opinion: English language proficiency and school performance of speakers of other languages in the United States. NABE News, 18,6: 17-19.

Laosa, L. 1975. Bilingualism in three United States Hispanic groups: Contextual use of language by children and adults in their families. Journal of Educational Psychology 67: 617-627.

Laosa, L. 1984. Ethnic, socioeconomic, and home language influence upon early performance on measures of abilities. Journal of Educational Psychology 76: 1178-1198.

Lopez, D. 1978. Chicano language loyalty in an urban setting. Sociology and Social Research 62:267-78.

McCarthy, K. and Valdez, R.B. 1985. Current and Future Effects of Mexican Immigration in California. Santa Monica, CA: The Rand Corporation,

McConnell, B. 1985. Bilingual education and language shift. In Elias-Olivares, L., Leone, E., Cisneros, R., and Gutierrez, J. (Eds.) Spanish Language Use and Public Life in the United States. New York: Mouton. pp. 201-215.

McQuillan, J. and Tse, L. 1995. Child language brokering in linguistic minority communities. Language and Education 9:195-215.

Merino, B. 1983. Language loss in bilingual Chicano children. Journal of Applied Developmental Psychology 4: 277-294.

Nielsen, F. and Lerner, S. 1986. Language skills and school achievement of bilingual Hispanics. Social Science Research 15: 209-240.

Pease-Alvarez, L. and Winsler, A. 1994. Cuando el maestro no habla Espanol: Children's bilingual practices in the classroom. TESOL Quarterly 28: 507-535.

Perdraza, P. and Pousada, A. 1992. Bilingualism in and out of school: Ethnographic perspectives on the determination of language "dominance." In M. Saravia-Shore and S. Arvizu (Eds.) Cross- Cultural Literacy. New York: Garland, pp. 253-272.

Pucci, S. 1994. Supporting Spanish language literacy: Latino children and free reading resources in schools. Bilingual Research Journal 18: 67-82.

Rodriguez, R. 1982. Hunger of Memory: The Education of Richard Rodriguez. New York: Bantam Books.

Romo, H. and Falbo, T. 1996. Latino High School Graduation: Defying the Odds. Austin: University of Texas Press.

Skrabanek, R. 1970. Language maintenance among Mexican-Americans. International Journal of Comparative Sociology 11: 272-282.

Sole, C. 1982. Language loyalty and language attitudes among Cuban-Americans. In J. Fishman and G. Keller, (Eds.) Bilingual Education for Hispanic Students in the United States. New York: Teachers College Press. pp. 254-268.

Tienda, M. and Neidert, L. 1984. Language, education, and the socioeconomic achievement of Hispanic origin men. Social Science Quarterly 65: 519-536.

Tse, L. 1995. Language brokering among Latino adolescents: Prevalence, attitudes, and school performance. Hispanic Journal of Behavioral Sciences 17: 180-193.

Tse, L. 1996. Language brokering in linguistic minority communities: The case of Chinese- and Vietnamese-American students. Bilingual Research Journal 20 (3,4): 485-498.

Turbak, G. 1994. Let's hear it in English. Reader's Digest 145, number 869, September, 1994: 177-180.

Veltman, C. 1983. Language Shift in the United States. Berlin: Mouton.

Waggoner, D. 19839. Spanish language futures in the US: A methodological critique. NABE Journal 13: 253-261.

Wong Fillmore, L. 1991. When learning a second language means losing the first. Early Childhood Research Quarterly 6: 323-346.

Chapter Eight:
Inoculating Bilingual Education Against Attack

Opposition to bilingual education has never been more intense. I would like to suggest a simple means of overcoming this problem: Make bilingual education so successful that there is simply no doubt of its effectiveness.

While bilingual education is doing very well, it can do much better. In my opinion, bilingual programs will not realize their true potential unless they do a much better job of providing a print-rich environment in the primary language, and encouraging children to read. The case for reading in bilingual education rests firmly on theory and research. As discussed in chapter one, successful bilingual education provides the following:

1. Comprehensible input in English (ESL, sheltered subject matter teaching)
2. Subject matter knowledge, from classes taught in the primary language.
3. Literacy development in the primary language.

ESL and sheltered subject matter classes provide comprehensible input directly, while subject matter teaching in the first language helps provide comprehensible input indirectly, supplying background knowledge that makes English input more comprehensible. Literacy developed in the first language transfers to the second.

We can add a fourth characteristic:

4. Continued development of the primary language, for economic, job-related advantages, and cognitive advantages.

Reading, especially free voluntary reading, can contribute enormously to each of these four aspects:

1. Reading is an excellent way of providing comprehensible input in English. A growing amount of research indicates that free voluntary reading contributes to second language reading ability, writing ability, vocabulary, grammatical competence, and spelling (e.g. Elley and

Mangubhai, 1983; Polak and Krashen, 1988; Tudor and Hafiz, 1989; Hafiz and Tudor, 1989, Elley, 1991; Pilgreen and Krashen, 1993; Cho and Krashen, 1994,1995a, 1995b; Constantino, 1994a; Lee, Krashen, and Gribbons, 1996.

2. Reading, done in any language, is an important source of knowledge. Those who read more, know more (e.g. Ravitch and Finn, 1987).

3. The power of reading for first language development is well-documented (Krashen, 1993): The best way of developing literacy in the primary language is thus through reading in the primary language.

4. It is safe to conjecture that those who have continued to develop their primary language read in that language.

There is, therefore, good reason to support reading in both the first language and the second language. Reading in the primary language can provide much of the "common underlying proficiency" (Cummins, 1981) that helps ensure English language development, and English reading will promote English language development directly. In addition, there is some evidence that a reading habit in the first language transfers to the second language: Flahive and Bailey (1993) reported a significant positive correlation between how much international university students read in their first language and in their second language. Thus, free reading in the first language may mean more reading, and hence more literacy development, in the second language.

Where are the Books? Not at Home

Books are very scarce in the lives of limited English proficient children. Ramirez, Yuen, Ramey and Pasta (1991) investigated the print environment in the homes of limited English proficient children participating in three types of programs in order to determine if the home print environment was a confounding factor in their study of program effectiveness. It was not. Children in all three programs had similar numbers of books in the home. What was remarkable, however, was the paucity of books in the homes of the children in all three programs: the average number of books in the home that were not schoolbooks was only 22 ("immersion" = 20.4 books; early exit = 23; late exit = 24). By way of comparison, it is not unusual for middle-class children to own 50 to 100 books of their own by the time they are adolescents. The Ramirez et. al. figure of 22 included all books in the home, not only children's books.

Where are the Books? Not at School

School has not helped to solve this problem. There is growing evidence that a relationship exists between the number of books available in school libraries and reading achievement (Elley, 1992; Lance, Welborn and Hamilton-Pennell, 1993; Krashen, 1995), a finding that makes good sense in light of other research showing that more reading takes place when children have more access to books (Krashen, 1993) and that reading itself is the source of literacy development. Elley's results are particularly relevant here: He found the clearest relationship between number of books in school libraries in less economically developed countries, countries in which the school library was probably the only source of books for children.

Pucci (1994) studied policies and book holdings in three school districts in Southern California. In one of the districts, schools could only buy books from a list of approved books. The maximum number of titles approved for Korean was 19 (17 fiction, 2 non-fiction), for Vietnamese 19 (18 fiction), and for Chinese 106 (68 fiction)! Pucci also examined library collections in nine schools that had a significant number of Spanish-speaking students. Table 8.1 presents some of her results (names of the schools used are fictitious).

Table 8.1.
Books in School Libraries

School	% Spanish L1	% LEP	Total books/child	Spanish bks/Spanish speaking child
Loma	95%	80%	2.3	.6
Estrella	98%	82%	3.6	.8
Alvarado	90%	82%	2.2	.5
Lily Ave	30%	35%	4.7	.6
86th St	65%	65%	3.3	1.0
Homer Middle	85%	70%	3.9	.04
Arapahao Middle	92%	70%	3.2	.12
Harbor	55%	50%	25.4	5.5
Cedar	88%	69%	5.3	1.0

from: Pucci, 1994

Inspection of table 8.1 shows that the total book holdings are inadequate: The national average for elementary school libraries is about 18 books per child (White, 1990), and nine out of ten schools in table 1 are well below this. (The exception, Harbor, is a small school, with a total enrollment of 375 children.) While the holdings in English are inadequate, the holdings in Spanish are pathetic.

Pucci also reported that access to the few books available was very restricted. Library visits ranged from once a week to once a month, with some teachers never bringing their students to the library. Library time ranged from 30 to 45 minutes, with a portion of that time for browsing and checking books out. In addition, "libraries at all schools have limits as to the number of books children are allowed to check out," with two books the maximum at all elementary schools, except for Alvarado, which allowed only one book! The middle schools allowed only three books per child every two weeks. In most elementary schools, however, children were allowed to check out more books if they returned the ones they had, provided they had the opportunity to use the library.

Pucci reported that "At Alvarado the atmosphere about checking out books was particularly tense, and the children's activity was noticeably regimented. Children browse the bookshelves holding a ruler, which they use to mark the place where they remove a book in order to examine it. They are not allowed to walk back to their table with the book. Rather, they must stand near the shelf and look at it there, deciding if they wish to check it out. Once children have chosen their books they go immediately to check them out and then sit quietly at their assigned seats. Many of them start reading, and finish their book before the end of the allotted library time is up. When this happens, they are not allowed to return the book and check out another. In fact, one third grade teacher was overheard strongly advising the children "not to read." (pp. 74-75).

A few children found a way of smuggling a little more reading into their lives, passing their books to their classmates and reading their classmates' choices first, and saving their own selections for later.

In Krashen (1993), I summarized research showing that libraries were a major source of books for children. In Pucci's study, this was also the case. She interviewed 159 children and asked them to identify their primary source of free-reading materials. 72% of the children named the school library and 19% the public library. Only 6% named teachers, and only 3% named parents, undoubtedly a reflection of the economic situation their families are in. (Pucci notes that "students who reported the teacher as the primary source are all from one class at Cedar, whose teacher was in a position to receive a large number of sample books from various publishers" (p. 77).

Do They Know about the Library?

It also appears to be the case that language minority students and their parents have little knowledge of the school library. Constantino (1994b) interviewed 14 high school students enrolled in intermediate ESL classes, and reported that use of the school library was rare and "not one of the students interviewed talked about the library as a source of pleasure reading" (p. 9). None of the students, except one, were aware that there were magazines and newspapers in the school library. Constantino (1995) reported that parents of language minority students are spectacularly uninformed about the libraries in general. Of 27 parents she interviewed, only one was aware of the function of the library and used it, and 24 out of the 27 "had absolutely no understanding of the library" (p. 10).

The situation is clear: reading causes literacy development, but these childen have little reading material in the home, and little in school. What little there is in school is not easily accessible, and limited English proficient students do not know much about what is available. Here is an analogy: I am putting you on a weight gaining/muscle building program. Your diet is one glass of water and a cracker each day. If you don't gain weight and get strong on this diet, it is your fault–you are just not trying hard enough. The problem is especially acute for middle school and junior high school students. It has been documented (e.g. Lamme, 1976; Tunnell, Calder, Justen, and Phaup, 1991) that interest in leisure reading begins to decline around grade four.

If bilingual education is doing well now, just think of how well it could do if children had access to reading, in both the first and second language. In some of our programs, children reach the 50th percentile on standardized tests at grade five, doing as well as native speakers in their own districts (Burnham and Piña, 1990). If we took school libraries and reading seriously, we could do even better: Our children would score in the 60th, 70th, 80th and 90th percentiles in language and reading and bilingual education would be inoculated against attack.

To do this, however, we need more than a token increase in the number of books in school libraries: We need a true "book flood." Recall that the average elementary school library in the United States supplies 18 books per child. For language minority children, who usually have few books available outside of school, this figure is a rock-bottom minimum.

References

Burnham-Massey, L. and Piña, M. 1990. Effects of bilingual instruction on English academic achievement of LEP students. Reading Improvement 27:129-132.

Cho, K.S. and Krashen, S. 1994. Acquisition of vocabulary from the Sweet Valley High series: Adult ESL acquisition. Journal of Reading 37: 662-7.

Cho, K.S. and Krashen, S. 1995a. Becoming a dragon: Progress in English as a second language through narrow free voluntary reading. California Reader 29, 1, 9-10.

Cho, K.S. and Krashen, S. 1995b. From Sweet Valley Kids to Harlequins in one year: A case study of an adult second language acquirer. California English 1,1: 18-19.

Constantino, R. 1994a. Pleasure reading helps, even if students don't believe it. The Journal of Reading 37, 504-5

Constantino, R. 1994b. Immigrant ESL high school students' understanding and use of the school and public library. SCOPE Journal 93: 6-18.

Constantino, R. 1995. Minority use of the library. California Reader 28: 10-12.

Cummins, J. 1981. The role of primary language development in promoting educational success for language minority students. In Schooling and Language Minority Students, ed. by State of California Department of Bilingual Education. Los Angeles: California State University. pp. 3-49.

Elley, W. 1991. Acquiring literacy in a second language: The effect of book-based programs. Language Learning 41: 375-411.

Elley, W. 1992. How in the World Do Children Read? Hamburg: International Association of the Evaluation of Education.

Elley, W. and Mangubhai, F. 1983. The impact of reading on second language learning. Reading Research Quarterly 19: 53-67.

Flahive, D. and Bailey, N. 1993. Exploring reading-writing relationships in adult second language learners. In Reading in the Composition Classroom, ed. by J. Carson and I. Leki. Boston: Heinle and Heinle. pp. 128-140.

Hafix, F. and Tudor, I. 1989. Extensive reading and the development of language skills. English Language Teaching Journal 43: 4-13.

Krashen, S. 1993. The Power of Reading. Englewood, CO: Libraries Unlimited.

Krashen, S. 1995. School libraries, public libraries, and the NAEP reading scores. School Library Media Quarterly 23: 235-237.

Krashen, S. and Biber, D. 1988. On Course: Bilingual Education's Success in California. Ontario, CA: California Association for Bllingual Education.

Lamme, L. 1976. Are reading habits and abilities related? The Reading Teacher 30: 21-27.

Lance, K., Welborn, L., and Hamilton-Pennell, C. 1993. The Impact of School Library Media Centers on Academic Achievement. Englewood, CO: Libraries Unlimited.

Lee, Y.O., Krashen, S. and Gribbons, B. 1996. The effects of reading on the acquisition of English relative clauses. ITL: Review of Applied Linguistics 113-114: 263-273.

Pilgreen, J. and Krashen, S. 1993. Sustained silent reading with English as a second language high school students: Impact on reading comprehension, reading frequency, and reading enjoyment. School Library Media Quarterly 22: 21-23.

Polak, J. and Krashen, S. 1988. Do we need to teach spelling? The relationship between spelling and voluntary reading among community college ESL students. TESOL Quarterly 22: 141-146.

Pucci, S. 1994. Supporting Spanish language literacy: Latino children and free reading resources in schools. Bilingual Research Journal 18: 67-82.

Ramirez, D., Yuen, S., Ramey, D. and Pasta, D. 1991. Final Report: Longitudinal Study of Structured English Immersion Strategy, Early-Exit and Late-Exit Bilingual Education Programs for Language Minority Students, Vol. I. San Mateo, CA: Aguirre International.

Ravitch, D. and Finn, C. 1987. What Do Our 17-Year-Olds Know? New York: Harper & Row.

Tudor, I. and Hafiz, F. 1989. Extensive reading as a means of input to L2 learning. Journal of Research in Reading 12:164-178.

Tunnell, M., Calder, J., Justen, J., and Phaup, E.S. 1991. Attitudes of young readers. Reading Improvement 28: 237-243.

White, H. 1990. School library collections and services: Ranking the states. School Library Media Quarterly 19: 13-26.

Appendix: Comments on a Recent Critique

Basing their conclusions on an analysis of 72 studies that they considered to be methodologically acceptable, Rossell and Baker (1996) conclude that the research evidence does not support transitional bilingual education as a superior form of instruction for limited English proficient children (p. 7). I was not able to re-examine all the studies Rossell and Baker cited, because most were unpublished reports. I did, however, read all of the studies they cited that appeared in the professional literature, and found numerous problems with Rossell and Baker's conclusions. I examine here studies in which submersion and "immersion" are claimed to be superior to bilingual education. I then discuss those studies Rossell and Baker categorized as "unacceptable."

Submersion versus Bilingual Education

Rossell and Baker conclude that in the case of English reading comprehension, transitional bilingual education was superior to submersion in 22% of the studies, worse in 33%, and there was no difference in 45% of the studies (60 studies were examined). Of the 20 studies in which submersion was claimed to be superior to bilingual education, two were in the published professional literature and I was able to get information on one other.

Moore and Parr, 1978: This study examined children in four programs: maintenance, transitional, minimal and English-only, and concluded that the latter group scored significantly higher than the others on tests of English reading. We are, however, given no details whatsoever on what went on the the bilingual classes; all we have are labels. In addition, the duration of the study was short: Moore and Parr's oldest subjects had just finished grade two. It typically takes longer for bilingual programs to show a positive impact on English language tests. In addition, no raw data is provided, so it is difficult to tell what the real effect of each program was.

Curiel, Stennina and Cooper-Stenning, 1980: In this study, seventh graders who had been in bilingual education were compared to comparison students who had not. While Rossell and Baker classify this study as showing submersion to be superior, this is not what Curiel et. al. report. For reading comprehension tests given in grade six, non-bilingual education students were significantly better. But at grade seven, there was no significant difference between the groups, although the comparison students were slightly better (mean = 6.35, compared to 5.98). In addition, students in bilingual education had significantly higher grade point averages and fewer of them were retained (30 out of 90 controls had been retained one year in elementary school, compared to 11 out of 86 bilingual education students). Finally, Curiel et. al. note that the bilingual program was used as a remedial program for some students who were previously placed in the monolingual English program .

Rossell and Baker complain that no one looks at the future educational success of graduates of bilingual or immersion programs (p. 41). Curiel and his associates attempted to do this. In Curiel, Rosenthal, and Richek (1986), students who were studied in Curiel et. al. up to grade seven, described just above, were followed to grade 11. (Rossell and Baker cite this study, but classify it as methodologically unacceptable.) In the follow-up, Curiel and associates report that students who had been in bilingual programs outperformed comparisons on all measures. While 12 of 90 comparison students had been retained in grades seven, eight and nine, only 4 out of 82 bilingual education students had been retained. Fewer bilingual education students dropped out of school (23.5%, compared to 43%). Bilingual students had higher grade point averages, but the difference was not significant (note that those who dropped out probably had lower grades.)

El Paso: Rossell and Baker include El Paso evaluations as studies showing submersion to be more effective than bilingual education. This is a bizarre analysis: neither program was a submersion program. Two programs were compared in El Paso. One, labelled "bilingual immersion" by the El Paso Unified School District, was clearly bilingual education. It contained a "native language cognitive development component" (NLCD), described by the El Paso Independent School District (1989b) as follows:

"NLCD is taught for 60 to 90 minutes per day. The objective of this component is to develop concepts, literacy, cognition, and critical thinking skills in Spanish. It is during this period that instruction and student-teacher interaction are entirely in Spanish. The more demanding content area concepts are also introduced during NCLD, particularly in the first grade (p. 54)."

This program employed the Natural Approach for ESL, a whole language approach to language arts, and sheltered subject matter teaching.

Thus, "bilingual immersion" in El Paso combined instruction in the first language with comprehensible input-based methodology, similar to the gradual exit variable threshold plan described in chapter 2.

The second program was also considered to be bilingual education, but differed in some important ways. Referred to as SB 477, it used a skills oriented approach:

It must be understood that BIP (bilingual immersion program) is not an English version of the SB 477 instructional program. SB 477 is built on a philosophy that advocates traditional concepts of teaching language ... SB 477 focuses the child's attention on the details of language such as phonetic sounds and grammar rules" (p. 9).

While bilingual immersion used whole language and Natural Approach activities, the most commonly used materials in SB 477 were basal texts and workbooks (El Paso Independent School District, 1987, p. 18). According to a 1989 report, whole language and comprehensible input-based methodology had been gradually introduced into SB 477 from 1985 to 1987, but observations indicated that the changes had not been fully implemented by SB 477 teachers (El Paso Independent School District, 1989a, p. 10).

Gersten, Woodward, and Schneider (1992) published a detailed report on the El Paso programs, limiting their analysis to students who had been in either program continuously. Gersten et. al. confirmed that the bilingual immersion students excelled in grade four in all aspects of academic performance, but by the seventh grade, no significant differences were found (p. 13). Far more bilingual immersion students, however, had been placed in the mainstream at grade 6, and more bilingual immersion teachers were confident about their students' eventual success in the mainstream.

Neither program was particularly successful, however. Sixth graders did acceptably well on the Language and Math Subtests of the Iowa Test of Basic Skills, but did poorly on the Reading Comprehension test, with bilingual immersion students scoring around the 23rd percentile and SB 477 students scoring at the 21st percentile. Vocabulary scores were even lower. The students themselves said that their hardest subjects were social studies and language arts, those which demand the most competence in academic English (pp. 25-26). In addition, even though bilingual immersion teachers were more confident of their students' eventual success in the mainstream, only 73% thought they would succeed in the regular program, and only 45% of the SB 477 teachers predicted success for their students. Gersten et. al. note that "These levels of performance, sadly, are typical for low-income Hispanic students in the junior high school years" (p. 29). This may be true, but as argued in chapter 8, I think we can do much better.

All we can conclude from the El Paso program is that a well-designed bilingual program was better than a less well-designed program up to grade four, with no differences (or a slight edge for bilingual immersion) by grade seven. Such studies will help us decide among bilingual education options, but do not address the issue of bilingual education versus submersion.

Berkeley: Rossell and Baker include a study by Rossell (1990) of LEP performance by children in Berkeley as showing that submersion plus ESL was, in one case, superior to bilingual education, and in another that there was no difference in English reading. The programs Rossell compared were labelled bilingual education and pull-out ESL, but no description of Berkeley's bilingual education program was provided, other than the fact that it was labeled bilingual education and that instruction was in Spanish 30 to 50 percent of the time.[1]

Immersion versus Bilingual Education

The term immersion has been used in a number of different ways. Here, I will focus on just two uses.

Canadian-style immersion (CSI): As is well-known, CSI is a program in which middle-class children receive much of their subject-matter instruction through a second language. Efforts are made to make sure the language they hear is comprehensible. Children in these programs learn subject matter successfully and acquire a great deal of the second language.

Consideration of the principles of bilingual education presented in chapter 1 leads to the conclusion that CSI is similar, if not identical, to bilingual education. Children in CSI receive comprehensible input in the second language and develop literacy and subject matter knowledge in their first language, both outside of school and in school; children in CSI are typically middle class, and do a considerable amount of reading in English outside of school (suggested by Cummins, 1977, and confirmed by Eagon and Cashion, 1988). Even in early total immersion programs, a great deal of the curriculum is in English, with English language arts introduced around grade two. By grade six, half the curriculum of early total immersion is in English. Most important, the goal of CSI is bilingualism, not the replacement of one language with another.

Structured immersion (SI): As described by Gersten and Woodward (1985), SI has these characteristics:

(1) Comprehensible subject matter instruction.
(2) Use of the first language when necessary for explanation, but this is kept to a minimum.

(3) Direct instruction of grammar.
(4) Pre-teaching of vocabulary.

While the first two characteristics are supported in the research literature, there is little evidence supporting the efficacy of direct grammar instruction (Krashen, 1994) and pre-teaching vocabulary has not been found to be consistently effective (Mezynski, 1983).

Rossell and Baker (1996) claim that immersion was more effective than bilingual education for English reading in eight studies. Information concerning six of these studies was available.

Barik, Swain and Nwanunoki (1977) and Barik and Swain (1978) are studies of Canadian-style immersion with French as the target language in which early total immersion is compared to partial immersion. In partial immersion, there is less teaching in French; from the beginning, some subjects are taught in English and some in French.

While Rossell and Baker are not fully explicit concerning why these studies were included, the idea seems to be that early total immersion is similar to all-English immersion for LEP children and partial immersion is similar to bilingual education. Since Barik et. al. and Barik and Swain show that children in early total immersion acquire more French than children in partial immersion programs, immersion, it is concluded, is better than bilingual education.

But Canadian early total immersion is not the same as an all-English immersion program for LEP children. In fact, both versions of Canadian-style immersion under consideration here, early total and partial immersion, are quite similar to bilingual education. As noted earlier, much of the CSI curriculum is in the first language, English, and children in these programs typically come to school with a great deal of literacy development in the primary language. Since children in both programs come to school so well-prepared, it is reasonable to expect that more exposure to the second language, French, will result in more acquisition of French, because what is heard and read is mostly comprehensible.

Many LEP children in the United States, however, do not come to school with these advantages. An all-second language curriculum will be much less comprehensible to them, even if carefully sheltered. While sheltering will clearly help, supplying background knowledge and literacy in the first language is a sure way to ensure that instruction in English will be comprehensible.

Rossell and Baker are clearly aware of this argument. They point out, in defense of their position, that Canadian-style immersion programs have worked for working class students as well as middle class students. A few reports of Canadian-style immersion programs for working class children have been published (e.g. Holobrow, Genesee, Lambert, Gastright and Met, 1987). While these children have done well, evaluations so far have been limited to grade two and below. Also, as Genesee (1983) notes, none of these children can be said to come from destitute or 'hard-core' inner-city areas (p. 30).

We thus know very little about how well working class children do in second language immersion programs and nothing about how well under-class children would do. What we do know is that children of lower socioeconomic background experience less print outside of school and that the richness of the print environment is related to literacy development (evidence cited in chapter 3.)

<u>Bruck, Lambert and Tucker (1977)</u> compared children in total immersion (CSI) to native speakers of French, and thus has no bearing at all on the issue of bilingual education versus immersion.

<u>Genesee, Holobrow, Lambert and Chartrand (1989)</u> is a comparison of fifth graders in partial immersion, early total immersion, and the performance of English-speaking children in a French school designed for native speakers of French. This third group, however, had methodology that was quite similar to the students in early total immersion, and the population of the school was largely English-speaking. In fact, Genessee et. al. refer to it as super-immersion. Super- immersion students and early total immersion students performed similarly on nearly all measures.

An additional group of a small number of English speaking students in a French school with fewer English-speaking classmates was compared to the super-immersion students; performance was similar, with the submersion students doing better only on oral tests. Again, it is not clear why this study is included and how it is supposed to show that structured immersion is better than bilingual education. In my analysis, all groups had the benefits of bilingual education, with first language development coming from school and from home. We also cannot use the French school–immersion comparison to claim that submersion is equivalent or superior to bilingual education because we have no idea how the English speakers were dealt with in classes in the French school, that is, how much comprehensible input in French they received, in school and outside of school (e.g. tutors).

In <u>Gersten (1985)</u>, it is claimed that more students in structured immersion scored at or above grade level on standardized tests than children in bilingual education. Gersten's study meets the methodological criteria set out by Rossell and Baker (see below), but is full of other problems.

- Sample size: Gersten compared only 28 structured immersion students to 16 students in bilingual education. Because Gersten does not provide actual scores for the bilingual group, we have no idea how close to grade level these students were (one cohort of Sl students scored at the 64th percentile, the other at the 65th percentile). It is possible that if only a few students had slightly different scores, the results could have looked very different.

- Duration: Gersten examined student performance at the end of second grade. Gersten included follow-up data on the Sl students, and they did very well, with one cohort scoring at the 65th percentile in reading at the end of grade four and the other scoring at the 78th percentile in reading at the end of grade three. Each cohort, however, consisted of only nine children!

- Control for socio-economic factors: As noted earlier, SES has a powerful effect on school performance. Gersten informs us that his Sl students were low income and that the school they attended had a high proportion of low income, low achieving students, who became eligible for Title I funds (p. 188) but provides no supporting evidence of any kind. Nor is SES information provided about the comparison students in the bilingual education program. Comparison children did not attend the same school the Sl children attended. (We do not even know the name or location of the school or district studied. All we know is that the school is on the West Coast.)

- Lack of information about the bilingual education program: We are only told that comparison students participated in bilingual education programs in the district. We have no idea what the quality of the program was, what methodology was used, etc.. In addition, the comparison (bilingual education) students in cohort ll included two speakers of Korean, two speakers of Vietnamese, and two speakers of Samoan or Thai. This implies that this mysterious district provides full bilingual education programs in all of these languages at least up to grade two. I know of no districts that are able to do this. Gersten did not include information on the linguistic background of the bilingual education students in the other cohort. Such data, he states, was unavailable.

Finally, Gersten notes that the number of LEP students in the school he studied is small; his analysis included all LEP children who were in the program for at least eight full months (p. 190). These children, thus, were among many English-speaking peers. We do not know what the linguistic environment was like for the children in the bilingual education program.

Everything is wrong with this study.

Pena-Hughes and Solis, (1980) is unpublished, but it is discussed in several published papers. It is a comparison of two programs in McAllen, Texas. While

Rossell and Baker label these programs "immersion" and "bilingual education," Willig (1985, 1987) classified the immersion group as bilingual education, noting that the immersion group had instruction in English in the morning and instruction in Spanish reading in the afternoon. In addition, the explicit goal of the immersion program was bilingualism–development of both languages.

Also, the group Rossell and Baker label "bilingual education" did not, apparently, have a good program. According to an article in the Wall Street Journal (Schorr, 1983), classes were conducted partly in Spanish and partly in English, suggesting concurrent translation, a method shown to be ineffective (Legarreta, 1979). What apparently happened in McAllen is that children in a good bilingual program outperformed children in a poor bilingual program.

"Unacceptable" Evidence for Bilingual Education

In this section, I review several published studies that were either not cited by Rossell and Baker or classified as "unacceptable". My conclusion is easy to state: The "unacceptable" or omitted studies either support bilingual education or are irrelevant. The criteria Rossell and Baker used to exclude studies are the following (pp. 14-15):

1. "The study did not compare program alternatives or assess educational outcomes." My interpretation of this criteria is that the study had to compare bilingual education to something else (the title of their paper is "The educational effectiveness of bilingual education." In their tables, they include, however, a comparison of "immersion" versus "ESL", which does not involve bilingual education and also include a comparison of two versions of bilingual education: transitional versus maintenance[2]).

2. "The study did not use randomly assigned students and made no effort to control for possible initial differences between students in different programs." This criteria, we will see, is one that is frequently violated in the "unacceptable" studies. I will argue, however, that the results of these studies are too strong to be ignored and that there is reason to hypothesize that this violation is not as serious as Rossell and Baker suggest it is.

3. "The study did not apply appropriate statistical tests."

4. "The study used a norm-referenced design." These studies typically compare bilingual education students to national norms. Rossell and Baker argue that this is not valid because one would expect limited English proficient children to show dramatic gains once they acquire some English and can show their

true competence on tests. Nevertheless, strong progress in comparison to norms is certainly consistent with the hypothesis that bilingual education is effective.

5. "The study examined gains over the school year without a control group." Without question, gains seen without a control group are much less convincing. But they are suggestive, especially when they are far beyond expectations.

6. "The study used grade-equivalent scores." While imperfect, outstanding results with grade-equivalent scores should not, in my opinion, be ignored.

7. "The study compared test results in different languages for students in different programs." All test results to be discussed in this paper are tests given in English.

8. "The study did not control for the confounding effect of other important educational treatments that were administered to at least one of the groups, but not all of them." If the bilingual group did better, but had other treatments, one cannot say for sure that bilingual education was responsible for the advantage.

"Unacceptable" but Suggestive Studies

In this section, I survey studies that were classified as unacceptable by Rossell and Baker but that, nevertheless, provide interesting information. As we will see, the requirement most frequently failed of the eight listed above is number 2, failure to randomize or control for possible initial differences. The studies are presented chronologically:

Kaufman (1968) is classified both as "acceptable" and "unacceptable" in Rossell and Baker, and is listed as showing TBE to be superior to submersion. Kaufman compared Spanish-speaking junior high school students who were randomly assigned to one of two groups in grade seven. The experimental group had instruction in Spanish reading. This group consisted of two subgroups, one having Spanish reading instruction for four times per week for two years, and the other for only one year. The control groups had art, music and health education during the time the experimental group had Spanish reading. Each experimental subgroup had its own control group from the same school. Both groups "received equivalent instruction in English" (p. 523).

Table A.1 presents test results for English vocabulary and reading (Durrell-Sullivan Reading Capacity and Achievement Tests) adjusted for pre-test differences. In every case, the experimental groups did better, but in no case was the difference statistically significant. Effect sizes were low in some cases, and modest in others. Thus, this study could be classified as being pro-primary language instruction or "no difference," depending on the analyst's view of statistical significance.

Kaufman's study failed one of Rossell and Baker's requirements for acceptability; test scores were presented as grade equivalent units, not as raw scores.

Table A.1.
Reading and Vocabulary Scores

	n	means: vocabulary	reading
Spanish reading: two years	31	5.51	5.65
Control	19	5.29	5.53
effect size		.31	.16
Spanish reading: one year	20	4.86	4.87
Control	25	4.83	4.57
effect size		.04	.47

effect size computed by SK

Rosier and Farella (1976) and Vorih and Rosier (1978) reported that children in a Navajo-English bilingual program at the Rock Point school had better attainment in English when compared to English-only schools on the Navajo reservation, and did better than previous cohorts at Rock Point who did not have bilingual education. The study did not utilize random assignment and did not attempt to control for pre-test differences. Rosier and Farella (1976), in fact, note that Rock Point averages had been higher than those in the other schools since 1963-64. They were still, however, two years below national norms. In addition, the Rock Point studies utilized grade-equivalent scores, another violation of the Rossell and Baker requirements.

The Rock Point scores are nevertheless very impressive: Fifth graders in Rock Point who had had bilingual education scored 5.0 in 1975 and 5.4 in 1976 (compared to previous cohorts' 3.9 and 3.8) and sixth graders in 1976 scored 6.6 in reading comprehension (compared to a previous cohort's 4.7). Clearly, something good was happening at Rock Point.

Baker and de Kanter (1983) have other criticisms of the Rock Point data. They note that both the bilingual education students at Rock Point and previous cohorts experienced a large jump in test scores between grades 2 and 6; this increase, thus, can not be attributed to bilingual education. Even so, the Rock Point attainments in grades five and six are high. In addition, Baker and de Kanter point out that different versions of the SAT test were used in different years. Again, this is a flaw, but again, the scores of the fifth and sixth graders are a clear improvement. Finally, Baker and de Kanter (1983) point out that some students without a full experience in bilingual education may have been included in an analysis of combined scores. The high attainments of the fifth and sixth graders cited here are not a result of this analysis.

Ferris and Politzer (1981) compared English language competence and school success in two groups of Spanish-speaking junior high school students. One group was born in Mexico and had completed at least three years of education in Mexico, in Spanish. The second group was born in the USA and had had all schooling in English. Ferris and Politzer reported no difference between the groups on an essay written in English, "except for minor differences" in favor of the US-born group on points of grammar (verb inflections, pronoun agreement; there was no difference between the groups for paragraph development, sentence boundaries, article agreement, possessives, clauses per T-unit, and average T-unit length).

Of great interest is the finding that the group that had had some education in Mexico had significantly higher grades in English (mean 3.17 out of 4 compared to 2.53), reported that they tried harder to get good grades, and reported more discussion with teachers about school work.

Gale, McClay, Christie, and Harris (1981) Gale et. al. compared Australian aboriginal children in all-English schools and children who had bilingual education (Gapapuyngu). The bilingual model presented by Gale et. al. did not utilize translation, and gradually shifted instruction into English, beginning with math and English literacy. Gapapuyngu language arts was maintained until grade four. When tested at grade five, there were no differences between the groups in English vocabulary and story retelling (fluency), and the English-only children were better on a cloze test. By grade seven, however, the bilingual education group was far better on tests of fluency, on a cloze test, on English composition, on tests of subtraction, multiplication and division, and tended to be better in reading (table A.2).

Table A.2.
Grade Seven Results: Gapapuyngu Study

Test	English only	Bilingual	Effect size
Vocabulary	51.5	49.5	.42
Fluency	111.1	132.7	.53
Reading	6.70	7.18	.40
Cloze	24.0	52.5	1.00
Essay	8.8	12.9	1.52

Effect sizes calculated from t-values in Gale et. al.
From: Gale et. al. (1981).

As Gale et. al. note, there were flaws. Rossell and Baker's criteria 8 was violated: English-only controls were previous cohorts, and Gale et. al. point out that other curricular developments had been put in place and that the community was "becoming more Europeanized" (p. 301), with greater exposure to English. In addition, estimates of validity were not done for the locally developed tests. Nevertheless, the results are very strong.

Lofgren and Ouvinen-Bierstam (1982) compared the achievement of Finnish-speaking students living in Sweden who participated in a bilingual program to other immigrant children and native speakers of Swedish. Table A.3 presents results at grade 3:

Table A.3.
Bilingual Education in Sweden

Test results at grade 3	Finnish children	Other immigrant	Swedish children
n	32-34	29-46	33-62
Swedish standardized achievement test	1.9	1.9	2.3
Swedish	2.7	2.4	2.9
Mathematics	2.9	2.7	3.0

from: Lofgren and Ouvinen-Bigerstam, 1982

This study was classified as "unacceptable" apparently because of the lack of random sampling or control for pre-treatment differences, use of grade level equivalent scores, and the lack of a Finnish-speaking control group. It must also be pointed out that the Swedish speaking comparison students in this study scored well below national norms, but the results are certainly suggestive.

Croft and Franco (1983) reported that Spanish speaking children in a bilingual education program in New Mexico made better gains on the CTBS than a comparison group in grades 1,2 and 3, gaining an average of .3 more than comparisons over 7 months. Bilingual education students also made significantly better than "expected" gains in grades 4, 5 and 6. Randomization was not used, and grade level equivalent scores were reported, both violations of Rossell and Baker's criteria.

Medrano (1983, 1986) was not cited in Rossell and Baker. Medrano's subjects were 278 Mexican-American children taught in bilingual and non-bilingual programs. Medrano reported that the bilingual group was slightly, but not significantly better in reading, and significantly better in math at grade 3 (Medrano, 1983) and grade 6 (Medrano, 1986), controlling for grade 1 CTBS scores.

Fulton-Scott and Calvin (1983) compared students in bilingual education with two forms of English-only: pull-out ESL and "integrated ESL" (with native speakers of English). In a cross-sectional design, Fulton-Scott and Calvin examined grades and total CTBS examination results in grades one and six. There were no significant differences for any of the measures in grade 1, but bilingual education students earned significantly higher grades in grade six and their CTBS scores in grade six were significantly higher than children in the pull-out class. Effect sizes for grade six (table A.4) are very large.

Table A.4.
ESL vs. Bilingual Education

grade	pull-out mean	sd	ESL integrated mean	sd	ESL bilingual education mean	sd
1	1.56	1.14	1.06	.39	1.46	.35
6	4.89	.77	6.02	.79	6.85	.73

Effect sizes:
bilingual vs. pull-out ESL = 2.05
bilingual vs. integrated = 1.04

This study used grade equivalent scores, and would thus not be considered acceptable by Rossell and Baker.

Mortensen (1984) is listed in Rossell and Baker as "methodologically unacceptable," apparently because subjects were not randomly selected and no pretest was used as a covariate (Rossell and Baker cite this study as Mortensen's 1980 dissertation, not as a published paper). Mortensen compared grade 4, 5, and 6 Spanish speaking students in two programs, a bilingual program with transitioning to English reading in grade 3, and a monolingual English program.

From the description provided, the bilingual program appeared to contain the three components considered to be characteristic of good bilingual programs (Krashen and Biber, 1988): literacy development in Spanish, instruction in Spanish in academic areas, and ESL.

Mortensen reported no difference between the groups on a "word attack" test, but the bilingual education students were significantly better on a test of comprehension skills (table A.5).

Table A.5.
Performance on Word Attack and Comprehension Tests in English

		Number of Word attack skills mastered		Comprehension skills mastered	
	n	*mean*	*sd*	*mean*	*sd*
Bilingual	65	19.6	6.2	8.6	5.4
English-only	55	18.1	9.5	4.3	4.0

word attack: t = .94, ns
comprehension: t = 4.79, df = 105; effect size = .894
from: Mortensen, 1984

de la Garza and Medina (1985) is listed as an "acceptable" study in Rossell and Baker's bibliography but is not included in their analysis (they list it incorrectly as de la Garza and Marcella). de la Garza and Medina compared children in bilingual education to English-dominant children in an all-English program. Eighty percent of the bilingual education children were classified as "limited English proficient." The results were quite spectacular (table A.6).

Table A.6.
Results of English Language Testing

	Vocabulary		Reading Comprehension	
	Bil. Ed.	English	Bil. Ed.	English
n	24	118	25	117
Grade 1	47.74	49.89	50.29	49.58
Grade 2	55.23	51.40	52.90	51.29
Grade 3	52.53	50.57	51.89	50.35

from: de la Garza and Medina, 1985

The children in the bilingual program scored as well as the English speaking comparison students and even outperformed them in the second grade vocabulary test. In addition, the SES of the English speaking children may have been higher (37% free lunches versus 76%; Medina and de la Garza, 1989).

There are flaws in the study: The controls in this study were not limited English proficient but were categorized as English-speaking. Students in the bilingual classes "volunteered to participate" (p. 116), and only 25 subjects of the original 76 had test scores available for all three years (24 for vocabulary). Nevertheless, the results are amazing and cannot be ignored.

So (1987) was a secondary multiple regression analysis of questionnaire data, from the High School and Beyond data base. So analyzed questionnaire results of students who had Spanish as their mother tongue and who had to take ESL classes. Students were divided into three categories based on their report of their education in grades 1 through 6: those whose education was all or almost all in English, all or almost all in Spanish, or "evenly mixed English/Spanish." Regardless of SES, those in the "evenly mixed" classes did better on tests of reading achievement. For low SES, all Spanish was better than all English, but for other levels of SES all English was better than all Spanish. Once again, however, mixed Spanish/English was better than both of the other treatments.

Few bilingual programs in the US are conducted entirely in Spanish. Thus, a plausible reason for the lower performance of the all-Spanish group is that this group probably represents a large number of recent immigrants who simply have not had suffient time to acquire a great deal of academic English.

Krashen and Biber (1988), a report on bilingual programs in several school districts in California (Baldwin Park, San Jose, Fremont, Rockwood, San Diego), an individual school (Eastman), and a pre-school program (Carpinteria), clearly fails Rossell and Baker's criteria because random assignment was not used, nor were possible pre-exisiting differences in student achievement measured and controlled. In addition, statistical tests were not used. Once again, however, the results are solidly in favor of bilingual education.[3]

Gonzales (1989) used a design similar to the one used by Ferris and Politzer (1981). (Rossell and Baker cite Gonzales' dissertation, not the published report cited here.) He compared test performance of 34 sixth graders who had had at least two years schooling in Mexico and 38 sixth grade Spanish-speaking students who were born in Mexico but who had had all of their schooling in the United States. Both groups were enrolled in a bilingual program, but Gonzales' "Mexico" group had more literacy and subject matter instruction in Spanish. Table A.7 presents scores on a test of English literacy and an oral test of English.

Table A.7.
Performance on Tests of English

test	Mexico		USA	
	mean	sd	mean	sd
English reading	60.32	.12.70	53.05	17.04
English conv.	5.03	1.77	5.21	1.21

effect size for English reading: .48
Mexico: at least two years schooling in Mexico
USA: all schooling in USA
from: Gonzales, 1989.

The children who had had two years study in Mexico were slightly behind in English conversation, but both groups did very well: A perfect score on the test (the Bilingual Syntax Measure) is six. This confirms previous research showing that these children typically develop high levels conversational competence in English.

The Mexican group did significantly better than the USA group in English reading (Stanford Achievement Test), as well as on a test of Spanish reading. In addition, as others have found (see chapter 3), those who read better in Spanish also read better in English (r = .55). Thus, more instruction in the primary language did not hurt: It helped.

An earlier version of <u>Burnham-Massey and Piña (1990)</u> was included as part of Krashen and Biber (1988). It is a report of bilingual education in the Baldwin Park Unified School District in California. The program in Baldwin Park comes close to the characteristics of optimal bilingual programs, as described in Krashen and Biber. Children in the bilingual program scored about as well as native speakers of English in their district on the CTBS (table A.8).

Table A.8.
Long Term Results: Baldwin Park

test	group	grade 7	grade 8
CTBS Reading	Bilingual	35	38
	English	35	41
CTBS Language	Bilingual	56	46
	English	45	47
CTBS Math	Bilingual	61	63
	English	57	53

from: Burnham-Massey and Pina (1990)

Students in grades 7 and 8 had slightly higher grade point averages than the comparison students and outscored them on local tests of English reading, writing and mechanics. High school grades were equally impressive.

This study has the usual flaws: there was no comparison to limited English proficient children in an all-English program; comparison students were native speakers or English-dominant bilinguals. Also, the sample sizes in grades 7 and 8 were smaller than those reported in an analysis of the same cohorts in grade 5 (44 in grade 8, compared to 115 in grade 5 for the bilingual group), suggesting a selection bias. The results clearly show, however, that graduates of bilingual programs can do well.

Verhoeven (1991), not included in Rossell and Baker, studied 138 "working class" second grade Turkish-speaking children acquiring Dutch in the Netherlands. Several groups were studied. The first group consisted of two treatments: In grade 1, the submersion group first had instruction only in Dutch, the second language, followed by some instruction in Turkish literacy "for some hours per week". The transitional literacy group had Turkish literacy instruction along with oral Dutch. One subgroup continued with literacy instruction in both languages, adding Dutch after two months, while the other had only Turkish literacy until grade 2.

The second group "also followed a two-year transitional literacy curriculum" (p. 67).

In table A.9, I present Verhoeven's results for reading comprehension tested in Dutch, the second language, at grade 2. Note that both transitional literacy groups outperformed the submersion children. Statistical analysis showed that the scores were not significantly different, but children from the transitional class were better. (The effect size for the advantage of group 1 over submersion was a modest .38. For group 2 it was a more substantial .79).

Table A.9.
Results: Reading Comprehension in Dutch after Grade 2

group	n	mean	sd
L1 literacy- Group 1	25	13.44	3.6
L1 literacy- Group 2	38	15.21	4.2
Submersion	74	11.93	4.1

from: Verhoeven, 1991

In table A.10, I present Verhoeven's results for attitudes toward reading. Questions on this measure dealt with preference among school subjects, frequency of library vists, and free-time activities. Children who were in the transitional literacy program (only group 1 was tested) had significantly better attitudes toward reading in both Dutch and Turkish. If better attitudes and more interest in reading mean more reading, and if more reading means more literacy, these are important results.

	Dutch		Turkish	
	mean	sd	mean	sd
L1 literacy	12.00	2.4	12.89	1.5
Submersion	10.91	3.5	11.66	2.7

Table A.10.
Attitudes Toward Reading

from: Verhoeven, 1991

Consistent with studies done in other languages, Verhoeven also reported a significant correlation between reading ability in Turkish and Dutch: Those who read better in their first language also read better in their second language.

Table A.11 summarizes our results thus far, listing all published studies that violated the selection criterion. Ten studies are positive (bilingual education superior), one shows no difference, and none are negative (all studies in Krashen and Biber other than Burnham-Massey and Piña are counted as one study). If we add Medrano (1983, 1986) and Fulton-Scott and Calvin (1983), the scorecard changes to eleven positive, two no difference, and no negative.

Comments on Experimental Design

How serious is the failure to use randomization or the failure to control for possible pre-existing differences? In my view, it is important to note this flaw, but there are reasons to hypothesize that it is not fatal.

First, we have no reason to suspect that there were important differences among the groups; Mortensen (1984) reports that the children in her study all lived fairly close to each other and were of a homogeneous socioeconomic background and Ferris and Politzer (1981) report that the socioeconomic status of their Mexican-educated group was actually lower than their all US-educated group.

Table A.11.
Published Studies that Failed to Randomize or Otherwise Control for Pre-Existing Differences in Subjects.

Study	Other Flaw(s)	Results
Kaufman, 1968		No difference
Rock Point, 1976, 78	GE scores, Norm-ref.	Positive
Ferris & Politzer, 1981		No difference
Gale et. al., 1981	Possible confounds	Positive
Lofgren & Ouvinen-Begerstam, 1982		Positive
Croft & Franco, 1983	GE scores	Positive
Mortensen, 1984		Positive
de la Garza & Medina 1985	Compared to "English-speaking" children	Positive
So, 1987		Positive
Krashen & Biber, 1988	Other treatments Norm-ref.	Positive
Gonzales, 1989		Positive
Burnham-Massey & Piña, 1990	Compared to "English-speaking" children	Positive
Verhoeven, 1991		Positive

GE = grade equivalent scores used
norm-ref. = students compared to native-speaker norms

Second, one can argue that with a large number of studies, randomization is present. If we look at many studies with non-random assignment, and have no reason to believe that subjects in different treatments differ in relevant ways, it can be argued that randomization of subject assignment has, in fact, occured, because of the large number of studies. In other words, many slightly flawed studies can be combined to arrive at a valid analysis. In situations where randomization or pretesting are not possible, the answer is to use a post-test only design and to replicate many times.

Third, there is no evidence of selection bias in studies in which pre-test scores are available, that is, there is no consistent tendency for children placed in bilingual education to have higher pre-test scores.

- In Gersten (1985), in one cohort first-grade children in bilingual education scored 2.6 on the LAS for oral English, while English-only first-graders scored 2.7. In a second cohort, the respective scores were 2.28 and 2.18.

- Legarreta (1979) compared kindergarten children in submersion, submersion plus ESL, concurrent bilingual, concurrent bilingual with ESL, and bilingual without concurrent translation. Groups were not randomly assigned. Although all children were "identified as essentially monolingual in Spanish" (p. 524), the children in the concurrent translation plus ESL were lower in oral English comprehension at the start of the study. There were no differences among the other four groups.

- In Curiel, Rosenthal, and Richek (1986), there were no differences between students in bilingual education and English-only with respect to parents' education and books in the home. Students in the bilingual program spoke less English in the home.

- In Fulton-Scott and Calvin (1983) there was no significant difference among ESL and bilingual education children in CTBS scores in grade one.

In these studies, at least, there was no bias in favor of bilingual education.

Other Flaws

In the first two sections of this report, I point out that some of the studies classified as "acceptable" by Rossell and Baker had serious problems. While they satisfied the requirements Rossell and Baker list, they had other problems. Do the "unacceptable" studies have these problems?

Sample size: I faulted Gersten (1985) because it compared 28 immersion children to 16 bilingual education students. The studies here contain more subjects. In addition, Gersten's measure (number of students who scored at or above grade level) makes the sample size problem severe, because a slight change in the scores of just a few students could have changed the overall results drastically.

Duration: Bilingual education often does not show its effects in early grades. Those studies in the "unacceptable" group that examined long-term achievement (Gale et. al., Mortensen, Gonzales, the Rock Point study, Burnham-Massey and Piña) show positive effects of bilingual education while in the studies with shorter treatments the effects seem to be smaller (Verhoeven, Kaufman, Medrano, 1983). It should be noted, however, that de la Garza and Medina found strong effects in very early stages, Ferris and Politzer's study of junior high school students showed no difference, and Medrano's 1986 follow-up study found no difference for English reading (but a significant difference for math, favoring bilingual education).

Control for socio-economic factors: SES was not explicitly controlled in all the studies discussed here, but there is no reason to believe groups differed remarkably in this aspect. In Gersten (1985), experimental and control subjects came from different schools and might have had different amounts of English spoken in their environment.

Lack of information about the bilingual program: Several authors were explicit about the bilingual programs. Some appeared to be at least fairly consistent with current views on optimal programs (Gale et. al., Rock Point, Mortensen, Krashen and Biber) while others were not (Kaufman, Lofgren and Ouvinen-Birgerstam). The former group reported better results, but these were also the longer-term programs. Gersten (1985) tells us nothing about "bilingual education" in his study.

Irrelevant Studies

A number of studies were categorized as "unacceptable" by Rossell and Baker, but were actually irrelevant to the purpose of their analysis. Their analysis was intended to focus on the effectiveness of TBE (transitional bilingual education) as shown by program evaluations. But some of the studies listed had very different goals:

Parr, Baca, and Dixon (1981) compared individualized and group instruction in a bilingual education setting. It did not compare bilingual education to non-bilingual approaches or to approaches utilizing less of the primary language. (They reported no difference between the two treatments.)

Chan (1981) is a comparison of Chinese-medium middle schools and bilingual (English-Chinese) schools in Hong Kong. No test scores for English language proficiency were included.

Ramirez and Politzer (1975) is not a program evaluation, but is an analysis of language use and language proficiency in Spanish and English. Their results are interesting: They found that home use of Spanish among elementary school students was unrelated to English proficiency but was related to Spanish proficiency, suggesting that use of Spanish at home was not harmful to English. Use of English at home, on the other hand, resulted in poorer Spanish but was of no value to English proficiency.

Collier (1987) did not compare bilingual education with another program. Collier investigated the effect of age of arrival and length of residence in the United States among immigrant children who were not in bilingual education programs and concluded that it took from four to eight years to reach average levels on academic tests.

Escamilla and Medina (1993) reported on the impact of a bilingual education program on "limited" language proficient children (some oral ability in either English or Spanish) and "most- limited" language proficient children (low oral ability in both English and Spanish). It was not a comparison of bilingual education with other options. It did, however, address the issue of what to do with children who seem to lack competence in both languages. The good news is that both groups gained in oral competence in both languages. 94.5% of the most-limited students and 85.8% of the limited students gained in English oral ability over a three year span (K-2).

Truly Unacceptable Studies

In some cases, Rossell and Baker are, in my view, correct in categorizing studies as "unacceptable," which means we learn nothing from them.

Golub (1978) claimed to be an "evaluation design" but had no control group and gave no scores on tests.

Trevino (1970) also had no control group and did not test for language.

Muller, Penner, Blowers, Jones, and Mosychuk (1977) is a comparison of children who participated in a Ukranian-English (50-50) bilingual program and comparisons who were randomly selected from a group of students with similar socioeconomic backgrounds who were not in the program. Muller et. al. found no differences between the groups at the end of grade one in English language development. This study was probably classified as "unacceptable" because participation in the experimental group was not determined randomly nor was there any control for pre-existing differences. I would also classify this study as unacceptable: It is not clear whether it is a study of bilingual education or heritage language development. Only eight of the 20 students in the bilingual program came from homes in which both parents used Ukranian in speaking to the child, and it is not clear, even in these cases, what level of competence the child had in Ukranian.

Balinsky and Peng (1974) had no control group of children not in bilingual education, and used a translation approach (each lesson taught twice), which explains why their childrens' gains were low: for second graders, about 1-2 months gained in English reading in six months time.

Conclusions on "Unacceptable" Research

Many of the published studies listed by Rossell and Baker as "unacceptable" are, to be sure, somewhat flawed, but a great deal can be learned from them. Despite the flaws, they are useful, and their consistent results cannot be ignored. In fact, the only published study in the unacceptable list that was negative was one I would also classify as unacceptable: Balinsky and Peng (1974), discussed just above.

A few studies were irrelevant. Their inclusion in the list of unacceptable studies gives the reader the impression that there are more unacceptable studies than there really are, and that the literature is of poorer quality than it really is. Interestingly, two of these studies provide evidence that supports bilingual education in other ways.

The Final Score

Combining the acceptable and unacceptable studies discussed here, my final tally is as follows: 12 studies support bilingual education, 4 show no difference, and 2 are negative. Both negative studies are short-term (Moore and Parr; Gersten) and in both cases no description is given of the bilingual program. Of the four studies showing no difference, bilingual education is not described in any detail in two (Medrano, Rossell).

We should also consider the fact that method comparisons are not the only evidence we have supporting bilingual education. We have independent evidence that the principles underlying bilingual education are correct: There is strong evidence that background knowledge makes input more comprehensible (see Krashen, 1985 for a review) and that literacy transfers across languages (chapter 3, this volume). In addition, as argued elsewhere (chapter 2, this volume), the hypothesized principles underlying effective bilingual education predict quite accurately why some people appear to be successful without bilingual education. This is powerful triangulation.

Notes

1. Rossell's report merits detailed discussion because of the importance attached to its conclusion in the popular press and the role it played in a court

decision (Teressa P. et al v. Berkeley Unified School District; US District Court, Case no. C-37-2346, DLJ).

To see how participation in a bilingual program affected performance, tables N.1, N.2 and N.3 present the regression coefficients computed by Rossell for participation in bilingual education. In all cases, relevant confounds such as

Table N.1.
Regression Coefficients in Rossell (1990) for Participation in Bilingual Education

Gains in test scores		All Subjects, includes Chance Scores				Actual Number Tested			
		BEd	se	t	n	BEd	se	t	n
Test	Years								
IPT, K-12	86-87	.522	.338	1.54	326				
IPT, K-6	86-87	.195	385	.507	250				
CTBS reading	86-87	-2.83	6.63	-.427	111	1.90	6.10	.311	85
CTBS language	86-87	-1.65	6.52	-.253	112	6.92	6.40	1.08	85
CTBS math	86-87	3.85	8.49	.454	120	5.28	7.67	.688	89
CTBS reading	87-88	-11.95	4.98	- 2.40	207	.626	4.42	.140	152
CTBS language	87-88	-13.24	5.37	-2.47	177	-3.63	4.99	-.727	152
CTBS math	87-88	-14.70	6.15	-2.39	208	-5.88	5.17	-1.14	154

BEd: regression coefficient for participation in bilingual education.
For sample sizes this large, t = 1.65 required for .05 level, one tail; t = 1.29 for .10 level.

socio-economic status (reflected by father's occupation) and age of students are controlled. The IPT is the IDEA Proficiency Test, which is given in the fall to all students considered potentially limited English proficient (Rossell, p. 86) in grades K through 12. The CTBS is administered in the spring, grades K-8 to students who score above a certain level in the IPT. For CTBS gains in table N.1, Rossell provides two sets of regression coefficients. The second set is based on the actual number of students tested, and is included in her paper in an appendix. The first set is based on more subjects; Rossell entered chance scores on the CTBS for those students who, on the basis of their IPT scores, were not eligible to take the CTBS at the start of the time span studied. In other words, gains are based on chance scores for the first analysis and actual scores for the second analysis of the CTBS.

From table N.1, it is clear that most of the regression coefficients are not statistically significant. As Rossell notes, the coefficients are significantly negative for gains on CTBS scores using the larger sample, suggesting that those who participated in bilingual programs gained less than those who did not. (Note, however, that there is evidence of a slight superiority for bilingual education for IPT scores for students in grades 1-12; the regresson coefficient for participation in bilingual education is positive and reaches the .10 level for a one-tail test. Rossell would probably call for a two-tailed test here, however.) It is very interesting that these negative results are reduced and sometimes disappear when the smaller sample is used, however.

Table N.2.
Performance of reclassified students

Measure	Years	BEd	se	t	n
CTBS reading	80-87	2.97	5.86	.508	301
CTBS language	80-87	5.81	7.32	.793	296
CTBS math	80-87	12.22	7.42	1.65	302
Grades, reading	80-87	1.30	.847	1.53	347
Grades, language	80-87	1.03	.864	1.19	289
Grades, math	80-87	.052	.849	.060	354

In another analysis (see table N.2), Rossell compared California Test of Basic Skills (CTBS) scores for bilingual and ESL pull-out students after "reclassification." Rossell concluded that these data showed no difference between the two groups. For each subtest of the CTBS, however, the regression coefficient for participation in bilingual education was positive and in the case of math, it reached the .05 level for a two-tailed test, which Rossell did not indicate, and for reading grades the t-value reached the .10 level of significance, one-tail.

Rossell also compared Berkeley LEP children's performance on California Assessment for Progress (CAP) tests to performance by LEP children in two districts considered to have "exemplary" bilingual programs, Fremont and San Jose (Krashen and Biber, 1988). Rossell reported no significant difference among the children in the three districts in reading, and reported that the Berkeley students excelled in math.

There are problems with this conclusion. First, this analysis does not compare gain scores nor does it show how rapidly children reach norms. It considers LEP children as a group. The comparison is only valid if, in fact, LEP children in all three districts entered their respective systems at the same level of competence, and if all three districts used similar criteria for exiting children. This may not be the case. According to Rossell's analysis of reclassified children in Berkeley, many children scored very well on the CTBS long before they were exited - in CTBS Reading, for example, children in ESL pull-out scored at the 33rd percentile two years before reclassification and at the 54th percentile one year before, while children in bilingual education who were reclassified scored at the 35th percentile two years before reclassification and near the 60th percentile one year before. CTBS Language Scores are similar, and scores in CTBS Math are even higher, with LEP children in Berkeley scoring above the 50th percentile four years before reclassification. Thus, Berkeley scores may look higher because some high-scoring children were retained in these programs longer.

Table N.3. Comparison of 3 Districts					
Measure	Years	BEd	se	t	n
Reading CAP	85-87	11.82	11.58	1.02	108
Math CAP	85-87	2.357	12.335	.191	108

n = number of schools
from: Rossell, 1990, tables 4.18, 4.19

Even if the analysis were a valid one - if children in all three districts entered at the same level and all three districts had equal reclassification criteria, it is interesting that, accoding to Rossell's analysis, schools that had bilingual education reported slightly higher CAP scores. Rossell's regression coefficients for bilingual education are presented in table N.3. The regression coefficients for bilingual education were positive (but did not reach statistical significance).

We are thus left with this picture of Berkeley: We have no idea how bilingual education was done in this district. According to one measure, Berkeley bilingual education students do not do as well as non-bilingual education students, but according to another (reduced sample) they do about as well (better in some measures, worse in others) Reclassification data gives bilingual students an edge, as does a comparison of LEP students across districts. This data hardly provides strong counterevidence to bilingual education.

2. The transitional vs. maintenance bilingual program study cited in Rossell and Baker is Medina and Escamilla (1992). TBE (transitional bilingual education) students (n = 125) were Vietnamese speakers; by grade 2, only 25% of their program was in the primary language. Maintenance students were Spanish-speaking (n = 298) and in grade 2, 60% of their program was in Spanish. There was evidence suggesting that the transitional students were of slightly higher SES: 55% of the transitional students received free or reduced price lunches, while 76% of the students attending the schools the maintenance students attended received free or reduced price lunches. Rossell and Baker claim that this study shows transitional bilingual education to be superior to

maintenance bilingual education in reading. This is not what happened. First, the measure used was oral language proficiency, not reading. Second, TBE was not superior. For the most limited students, there were no differences in gains in oral English. For the "nearly fluent," maintenance students were better both in kindergarten and grade 2. Superior gains were seen for the TBE students only in the most fluent group. Medina and Escamilla conclude that "results were mixed." (p. 282). In addition, the TBE students showed clear losses in their primary language, while the maintenance students did not.

3. Our report has been criticized by others as well. Chavez (1991) notes only that "the study of which (Krashen) is coauthor and which purports to demonstrate the practical effectiveness of keeping Hispanic children in extended bilingual programs is highly flawed. Moreover, it was published by the California Association for Bilingual Education, hardly a disinterested party in the debate" (p. 175). Chavez does not tell us what about the report is "highly flawed."

Imhoff (1990) maintains that the programs in Krashen and Biber (1988) worked because they were in "exemplary schools that are well-funded, staffed by highly trained and dedicated teachers, and composed of small classes of selected students" (p. 52). To my knowledge, not all of the schools described in our monograph were well-funded. The teachers did receive some extra in-service training in current theory and methodology, but to say they were more dedicated is not only unfounded but is also an insult to the teachers in the comparison groups. Nearly all of the students in the programs were unselected; there is no reason to suspect they differed from students in the comparison groups, and there is no reason to suspect differences in class size.

Rossell (1990) has also criticized our report, pointing out that one of the districts we studied, Fremont, took other positive action in addition to bilingual education (preschool, extra English reading, more parental involvement). While this could mean that these additional efforts were responsible for the Fremont children's outstanding performance, it is certainly not counterevidence to the hypothesis that bilingual education is effective.

Samaniego and Eubank (1991) raise several issues:

(1) Our analysis of Rockwood lacked controls. Thus, reported gains may not have been due to the treatment. But Rockwood students were compared to district norms (see our table 14). While district norms are not, strictly speaking, a control group, these comparison students had very similar backgrounds.

(2) They also were suspicious of a remarkable and "implausible" improvement made by Rockwood students (from the 6th to 38th percentile) from grades 3 to

6 in the 1981 cohort. Samaniego and Eubank claim that this result is even more remarkable because the sixth grade "had not even completed its first year of participation in the case study project" (p. 10). The project, however, began in Rockwood in 1981-82 and the sixth graders were tested in 1984.

(3) Their own analysis of data from Eastman and Rockwood led them to "strikingly different conclusions" (p. 10). Samaniego and Eubank compared sixth graders in Eastman in 1982, products of the old bilingual program, with 1986 sixth graders (who had received three years of instruction under the new plan) and found the median reading scores to be significantly different, in agreement with Krashen and Biber. In a similar analysis of Rockwood, however, Samaneigo and Eubank reported that the 1982 sixth graders were significantly better in reading than the 1986 sixth graders. The data reported in Samaniego and Eubank's monograph for Rockwood differs, however, from the data made available to us. For example, in Samaniego and Eubank's table 4, the 1986 sixth graders achieved a median reading score at the 25th percentile on CTBS Reading, but according to our data their mean score was the 39th percentile. (We were not provided with 1982 sixth grade scores.)

Samaniego and Eubank present regression analyses of the Eastman and Rockwood data that provide strong support for the hypothesis that reading ability transfers across languages. Performance on reading tests in Spanish was a significant predictor of sixth grade English reading in all analyses; in the Eastman school, Spanish reading alone was a significant predictor, while at Rockwood, it was significant in interaction with mathematics ability, tested in Spanish. Samaniego and Eubank did not investigate transfer of mathematics performance from the first to the second language. Their explanation is interesting: "... there is considerably less doubt about the ability to transfer technical knowledge ... There can be no doubt that bilingual education makes a strong and important contribution to the ultimate development of math skills in LEP students ... The evidence which shows this is so overwhelming that it seems to us unnecessary to provide an analysis (similar to the one done for language) ..." (pp. 42-43).

References

Baker, K. and de Kanter, A. 1983. Federal policy and the effectiveness of bilingual education. In K. Baker and A. de Kanter (Eds.) Bilingual Education. Lexington, MA: DC Heath. pp. 33-85.

Barik, H. and Swain, M. 1978. Evaluation of a bilingual education program in Canada: The Elgin study through grade six. Paper presented at the Colloquium of the Swiss Interuniversity Commission for Applied Linguistics. (ED 174 073).

Barik, H., Swain, M., and Nwanunobi, E. 1977. English-French bilingual education: The Elgin study though grade five. Canadian Modern Language Review 33: 459-475.

Balinsky, W. and Peng, S. 1974. An evaluation of bilingual education for Spanish-speaking children. Urban Education 9: 271-278.

Bruck, M., Lambert, W., and Tucker, G.R. 1977. Cognitive consequences of bilingual schooling: The St. Lambert Project through grade six. Psycholinguistics 6: 13-33.

Buriel, R. and Cardoza, D. 1988. Sociocultural correlates of achievement among three generations of Mexican American high school seniors. American Educational Research Journal 25:177-192.

Burnham-Massey, L. and Piña, M. 1990. Effects of bilingual instruction on English academic achievement of LEP students. Reading Improvement 27:129-132.

Chan, J. 1981. A crossroads in language instruction. Journal of Reading 24: 411-415.

Chavez. L. 1991. Out of the Barrio: Toward a New Politics of Hispanic Assimilation. New York: Basic Books.

Croft, D. and Franco, J. 1983. Effects of a bilingual education program on academic achievement and self-concept. Perceptual and Motor Skills 57: 583-586.

Cummins, J. 1977. Delaying native language reading instruction in immersion programs: A cautionary note. Canadian Modern Language Review 34: 46-49.

Cummins, J. 1981. The role of primary language development in promoting educational success for language minority students. In Schooling and language minority students. Sacramento, CA: California Department of Education. pp. 3-49.

Cummins, J., Swain, M., Nakajima, K., Handscombe, J. Green, D., and Tran, C. 1984. Linguistic interdependence among Japanese and Vietnamese immigrant students. In C. Rivera (Ed.) Communicative Competence Approaches to Language Proficiency Assessment: Research and Application. Clevedon, England: Multilingual Matters.

Curiel, H., Stenning, W., and Cooper-Stenning, P. 1980. Achieved reading level, self-esteem, and grades as related to length of exposure to bilingual education. Hispanic Journal of Behavioral Sciences 2: 389-400.

Curiel, H., Rosenthal, J., and Richek, H. 1986. Impacts of bilingual education on secondary school grades, attendance, retentions, and drop-out. Hispanic Journal of Behavioral Sciences 8: 357-367.

de la Garza, J. and Medina, M. 1985. Academic achievement as influenced by bilingual instruction for Spanish-dominant Mexican American children. Hispanic Journal of Behavioral Sciences 7: 247-259.

Eagon, R. and Cashion, M. 1988. Second year report on a longitudinal study of spontaneous reading in English by students in early French immersion programs. Canadian Modern Language Review 44: 523-526.

El Paso Independent School District. 1987. Interim report of the five-year bilingual-education pilot. 1986-1987 School Year. El Paso, Texas: El Paso Independent School District, Office for Research and Evaluation.

El Paso Independent School District. 1989a. Bilingual education evaluation: The fourth year in a longitudinal study. 1987-1988 School Year. El Paso, Texas: El Paso Independent School District, Office for Research and Evaluation.

El Paso Independent School District. 1989b. Bilingual education evaluation: The fifth year in a longitudinal study. El Paso, Texas: El Paso Independent School District, Office for Research and Evaluation .

Escamilla, K. and Medina, M. 1993. English and Spanish acquisition by limited-language- proficient Mexican Americans in a three-year maintenance bilingual program. Hispanic Journal of Behavioral Sciences 15:108-120.

Ferris, M.R. and Politzer, R. 1981. Effects of early and delayed second language acquisition: English composition skills of Spanish-speaking junior high school students. TESOL Quarterly 15: 263-274.

Fulton-Scott, M. and Calvin, A. 1983. Bilingual multi-cultural education vs. integrated and non- integrated ESL instruction. NABE Journal 7:1-13.

Gale, K., McClay, D., Christie, M., and Harris, S. 1981. Academic achievement in the Milingimbi bilingual education program. TESOL Quarterly 15: 297-314.

Genesee, F. 1983. Bilingual education of majority-language children: The immersion experiments in review. Applied Psycholinguistics 4:1-46.

Genesee, F., Tucker, G.R., and Lambert, W. 1978. An experiment in bilingual education: Report 3. The Canadian Modern Language Review 34: 621-643.

Gersten, R. 1985. Structured immersion for language minority students: Results of a longitudinal evaluation. Educational Evaluation and Policy Analysis 7:187-196.

Gersten, R. and Woodward, J. 1985. A case for structured immersion. Educational Leadership 43: 75-79.

Gersten, R., Woodward, J., and Schneider, S. 1992. Bilingual Immersion: A Longitudinal Evaluation of the El Paso Program. Washington, DC: The Read Institute.

Gonzales, L.A. 1989. Native language education: The key to English literacy skills. In D. Bixler-Marquez, J. Ornstein-Galicia, and G. Green (eds.) Mexican-American Spanish in its Societal and Cultural Contexts. Rio Grade Series in Languages and Linguistics 3. Brownsville, Texas: University of Texas - Pan American. pp. 209-224.

Golub, L. 1978. Evaluation design and implementation of a bilingual education program, grades 1-12, Spanish/English. Education and Urban Society 10: 363-383.

Holobrow, N. Genesee, F., Lambert, W., Gastright, J. and Met, M. 1987. Effectiveness of partial French immersion for children from different social class and ethnic backgrounds. Applied Psycholinguistics 8: 137-152.

Hoover, W. 1983. Language and literacy learning in bilingual instruction. Austin: Southwest Educational Development Laboratory.

Imhoff, G. 1990. The position of U.S. English on bilingual education. In C. Cazden and C. Snow (eds.) English Plus: Issues in Bilingual Education. Annals of the American Academy of Political Science. Newbury Park, CA: Sage Publications. pp. 48-61.

Kaufman, M. 1968. Will instruction in reading Spanish affect ability in reading English? Journal of Reading 11: 521-527.

Krashen, S. 1985. The Input Hypothesis. Beverly Hills, CA: Laredo Publishing Company.

Krashen, S. 1993. The Power of Reading. Englewood, CO: Libraries Unlimited.

Krashen, S. 1994. The input hypothesis and its rivals. In N. Ellis (ed.) Implicit and Explicit Learning of Languages. London: Academic Press. pp. 45-77.

Krashen, S. and Biber, D. 1988. On Course: Bilingual Education's Success in California. Ontario, CA: California Association for Bilingual Education.

Legaretta, D. 1979. The effects of program models on language acquisition by Spanish speaking children. TESOL Quarterly 8: 521-576.

Lofgren, H. and Ouvinen-Birgerstam, P. 1982. A bilingual model for the teaching of immigrant children. Journal of Multilingual and Multicultural Development. 3: 323-331.

Medina, M. and de la Garza, J. 1989. Initial language proficiency and bilingual reading achievement in a transitional bilingual education program. NABE Journal 13: 113-125.

Medina, M. and Escamilla, K. 1992. Evaluation of transitional and maintenance bilingual programs. Urban Education 27: 263-290.

Medrano, M. 1983. The effects of bilingual education on reading and mathematics achievement: A longitundinal case study. Equity and Excellence 21: 17-19.

Medrano, M. 1986. Evaluating the long-term effects of a bilingual education program: A study of Mexican American students. Journal of Educational Equity and Leadership 6(2): 129-138.

Mezynski, K. 1983. Issues concerning the acquisition of knowledge: Effects of vocabulary training on reading comprehension. Review of Educational Research 53: 253-279.

Moore, F., and Parr, G.. 1978. Models of bilingual education: Comparisons of effectiveness. The Elementary School Journal 79: 93-97.

Mortensen, E. 1984. Reading achievement of native Spanish-speaking elementary students in bilingual vs. monolingual programs. The Bilingual Review 11: 31-36.

Muller, L., Penner, W., Blowers, T., Jones, J. and Mosychuk, H. 1977. Evaluation of a bilingual (English-Ukranian) program. Canadian Modern Language Review 33: 476-485.

Parr, G., Baca, F., and Dixon, P. 1981. Individualized versus group instruction in bilingual education: A two year study. The Elementary School Journal 81: 223-227.

Porter, R. 1990. Forked Tongue: The Politics of Bilingual Education. New York: Basic Books.

Ramirez, A. and Politzer, R. 1975. The acquisition of English and the maintenance of Spanish in a bilingual education program. TESOL Quarterly 9: 113-124.

Rosier, P. and Farella, M. 1976. Bilingual education at Rock Point: Some early results. TESOL Quarterly 10: 379-388.

Rossell, C. 1990. The effectiveness of educational alternatives for limited-English-proficient children. In G. Imhoff (ed.) Learning in Two Languages. New Brunswick, NJ: Transaction Publishers. pp. 71-121.

Rossell, C. and Baker, K. 1996. The educational effectiveness of bilingual education. Research in the Teaching of English 30: 7-74.

Schorr, B. 1983. Grade school project helps Hispanic pupils learn English quickly. The Wall Street Journal.

Samaniego, F. and Eubank, L. 1991. A statistical analysis of California's case study project in bilingual education. Technical Report Series of the Intercollege Division of Statistics, University of California at Davis.

Smith, F. 1994. Understanding Reading (fifth edition). Hillsdale, NJ: Erbaum.
So, A. 1987. Bilingual education and hispanic reading achievement. Contemporary Education 59: 27-29.

Trevino, B. 1970. Bilingual instruction in the primary grades. Modern Language Journal 54: 255- 256.

Verhoeven, L. 1991. Acquisition of biliteracy. AILA Review 8: 61-74.

Vorih, L. and Rosier, P. 1978. Rock Point Community School: An example of a Navajo-English bilingual elementary school program. TESOL Quarterly 12: 263-69.

Willig, A. 1985. A meta-analysis of selected studies on the effectiveness of bilingual education. Review of Educational Research 55: 269-317.

Willig, A. 1987. Reply to Baker. Review of Educational Research 57: 363-376.

Index

Aguirre 44
Anderson 26
Arabic 25
    bilingual program 40
Asian 20
    speakers of Asian languages 59
Attinasi 44
Australian (aboriginal children) 83

Baca 93
Bailey 66
Baker 4, 33, 73-74, 76-87, 89, 92-94, 98
Baldwin 38
Baldwin Park (school district) 87- 88
Balinsky 95
Barik 28, 77
Barnes 38
Barrera 24
Bassano 15
Beard-Williams 51
Berkeley (school district) 76, 98
Berliner 38
Biber 47, 61, 88, 90, 93, 97-99
Biddle 38
Bills 55, 57-58
Books
    availability 66-68
    in the primary language 14
Bossers 27
Bruck 78
Bryant 38
Burmese 25
Burnham-Massey 69, 88, 90-91, 93

Calder 69
California 67-68, 87-88
Calvin 85, 90
Campbell 38

Canada 33-34, 37
    immersion (CSI) 76-78
Carpenter 25
Carroll 28
Carrow 55-56
Chall 38
Chan, J. 93
Chan, K. 38
Chandler 38
Chang 27
Christie 83
Chartrand 78
Chavez 46, 47, 99
Cho, Grace (case history) 17-18, 38
Cho, K-S. 66
Christison 15
Collier 94
Comprehensible input 3
Constantino 38, 66, 68-69
Cooper-Stenning 73-74
Crawford (*Hold Your Tongue*) 49, 58
Croft 85, 91
Cuba/Cubans 43, 52-54, 57
Cummins 10, 13, 27, 33-34, 39, 47, 51,
    60, 66
Curiel 73-74, 92

d'Andrea 52, 55
de Kanter 83
de la Garza 86, 87, 91
de la Pena 18
Devine 24
Diaz 52, 54-55
Diversity (classroom) 12
Dixon 93
Dolson 13
Dupuy 26
"Eastman Plan" 9

Elley 38, 65-67
Ellman 33
English
    as a second language (ESL) 36-37,
        60-61
    as official language 51
Escamilla 94, 98
Eubank 99
Eye fixation 25

Falbo 60
Farella 82
Feitelson 38
Fejgin 38-39
Fernandez 38, 62
Ferris 83, 87, 90-91
Feuerverger 14
Finn 66
Finnish speaking children living
    in Sweden 84
Flahive 66
Florida 54, 57
Forked Tongue by Porter 49
Franco 85, 91
Free reading 61, 66
Fremont (school district) 87, 97, 99
Fulton-Scott 85, 90

Gale 83-84, 91, 93
Garcia 52, 55
Gass 29
Genesee 78
Gersten 54, 75, 78-79, 92-93, 95
Ginsburg 33
Goldstein 38
Golub 94
Goodman 24, 38
Gonzales 87, 91
Gradual Exit Plan 9-16
Grammar (instruction) 77
Gray 25
Grenier 52, 54
Gribbons 45, 66
Guatamalans 47

Hakuta 52, 55
Hamilton-Pennell 38
Handscombe 27
Harrington 29

Harris 83
Hemphill 38
Hennelly 36
Herman 26
Hernandez-Chavez 58
Hodes 24
Hold Your Tongue by Crawford 49
Holobrow 78
Hong Kong 93
Hoover 27
Hosch 44
Hudelson 24
Hudson 58
Hudson-Edwards 55, 57
Hung 24
Hunger of Memory by Rodriguez 61

Imhoff 99
Immersion 76-80
Iowa 75

Jacobs 38
Japan 24-25
Just 25-26
Justen 69

Kaufman 81, 91, 93
Kim 45
Krashen 25-27, 38, 45, 47, 59-61, 66-68,
    77, 86-88, 91, 93, 95, 97, 99-100

Lambert 78
Lamme 69
Lance 38, 67
Languages
    other than English & Spanish:

    Chinese 25-26, 37, 62, 67, 93
    Dutch 23, 25-26, 85, 86
    French 26, 28, 77-78
    Gapapuyngu 83
    Hebrew 24-25
    Hmong 46
    Japanese 27, 37
    Korean 37, 45-46, 67
    Navajo 25, 55, 58, 82
    Pacific Island languages 59
    Polish 24
    Russian 5-6, 37
    Turkish 27, 89-90

Ukranian 94
Urdu 25
Vietnamese 27, 62, 67, 98
Yiddish 24
Yoruba 25
Laosa 51-52, 54
Lapkin 28
Laria 19
Lee, B. 45
Lee, S-Y. 24-25
Lee, Y-O. 66
Legarreta 80, 92
Lerner 62
Libraries 38, 67-69
Limited English Proficient (LEP) 9-16,
    51,100
Literacy
    transfer across languages 3-4, 23-31
    development 65-66
Lofgren 84, 91, 93
Lopez 5 2, 53
Los Angeles (school district) 34-35, 37, 39
Lucker 24

Mangubhai 65-66
The Manufactured Crisis by Berliner &
    Biddle 49
McArthur 58
McCarthy 57
McClay 83
McConnell 55-56
McDonald 29
McQuillan 49, 59, 62
Medina 86, 91, 93-94, 98
Medrano 85, 90, 93
Merino 55-56
Met 78
Mexican
    Americans 43, 52, 54-57, 59, 85
    children 47, 83
Mexico 88
Mezynski 77
Milne 33
Misplacement 46-47
Moore 73, 95
Mortensen 85, 90-91
Mullis 38

Nagy 26

Nakajima 27
NaturalApproach 48,74
Neidert 62
Netherlands 89-90
New York 35-37
Nielsen 38, 62
Nwanunoki 77

O'Brian 38
Ortiz 38
Out of the Barrio by Chavez 49
Ouvinen-Bierstam 84, 91, 93

Paris argument 5
Parr 73, 93, 95
Pasta 66
Pena-Hughes 79
Peng 95
Perez 19
Pease-Alvarez 54
Pedraza 55
Phaup 69
Pilgreen 66
Piña 69, 88, 90-91, 93
Polak 66
Politzer 83, 87, 90-91, 93
Porter 43, 47, 49
Pousada 55
Pucci 61, 67
Puerto Rican 54
Pull-Out ESL 12

Ramey 66
Ramirez 13, 66, 93
Ravitch 66
Raz 38
Reading
    & bilingual education 65-69
    strategies 25-26
    in the primary language 66
    & vocabulary scores 82
Reyes, Luis 36-37
Richek 74, 92
Rock Point School 91, 93
Rockwood (school district) 87
Rodriguez, Richard 19, 61
Romatowki 24
Romo 60
Rosenthal 33, 74, 92

Rosier 82
Rossell 4, 73-74, 76-78, 80-82, 85-87, 89, 92-99
Ruiz 28-29

Salvadoran 47
Samaniego 99-100
San Diego (school district) 87
San Jose (school district) 87, 97
Schorr 80
Schneider 54, 75
Shapiro 19
Sheltered subject matter teaching 6, 61, 74
Shin 45-46
Shu 26
Simpkins 44
Skrabanek 51-52
Snipper 43
Snow 38
So 38, 87, 91
Socio-economic status (SES) 1, 19, 33-39, 78
Sole 52-53
Solis 79
Stennina 73-74
Stevenson 24
Stigler 24
Structured Immersion ("SI") 76
"Submersion" 12, 73
"Super-immersion" 78
Swain 27, 77
Sweden 84

Taiwan 24, 25
Terrell 12
Texas 44, 52, 54, 56, 74-75
Tienda 62
Toronto 33-35, 37, 39
Torres 44
Trager 27
Tran 27
Transfer of Literacy 23-29
Transitional bilingual education (TBE) 93
Trevino 94
Tse 49, 55, 57, 62
Tucker 78
Tunnell 69
Turbak 51

Turner 19
Tzeng 24, 27

US English 49

Valdez 57
Variable Threshold 9-15
Veltman 52-53, 55, 57
Verhoeven 26, 27, 89-90
Vocabulary
    acquisition 26
    teaching 77
    & reading scores 82
Vorih 82

Waggoner 61
Wellborn 38, 67
White 67
Willig 80
Winsler 54
Woodward 54, 75
Wong 27
Wong-Fillmore 13, 58
"Word attack" 86
Writing, development of 25
Wu 25

Youssef 44
Yuen 66

Zhang 26